C000200952

# The Wisdom
# of
# Wormwood

## David Wilson

Being a compilation of the Wormwood column
published in Horsley's Over the Wall magazine
between the years 2004 to 2015.

Collected here for the first time, together with a
selection of additional material
from the same pen.

Published in 2020 by Over the Wall

ISBN: 978-1-8383117-0-4

Cover illustration:
Frank Spats was found on a deserted beach
near Windscale in West Cumbria
in the early 1970s

for

Mrs Wormwood

(you know who you are)

# Contents

# Acknowledgements

Most books have a section in which the author graciously thanks people who have offered help and encouragement and this one is no exception.

Firstly, I wish to acknowledge a debt of gratitude (immeasurable) to Nick Hackett, editor of Horsley's **Over the Wall** magazine[1], for his advice (invaluable), support (unstinting) and patience (unfailing) in putting up with last-minute trivial changes to my copy and, what is more, for pretending *that it really mattered*.

Then there are all the other people who contributed to the production of **Over the Wall** and helped deliver it to *every single household* in the village. You know who you are; to my shame, I confess, I'm not exactly sure.

Admirers of the Irish writer Flann O'Brien (1911-1966) may detect his influence from time to time in the following pages. I only hope it is not too obvious.

The other book that I find myself reading over and over again is the Jenguin Pennings by Paul Jennings. It is no longer in print but you should get yourself a copy if you find yourself enjoying Wormwood and feel ready to move on to *the real thing*.

And then of course there's Mrs Wormwood - my companion on life's road; you will meet her in the following pages.

---

[1] Now sadly defunct. Strange to think that there are people living in Horsley today for whom the days of Over the Wall are little more than a shadowy memory.

# Preface to the second edition

The first edition of The Wisdom of Wormwood was a purely electronic affair, available only on the various varieties of Kindle and covering the first eight years of Horsley's Over the Wall magazine.

With publication of this second edition (available both as a printed book and in Kindle format) readers can now enjoy all 48 of the Wormwood pieces together with a selection of additional material from the same pen.

Horsley,
November 2020

# Preface to the first edition

It must have been around Christmas, 2002 (can it *really* be that long ago?) that I got a phone call asking me if I'd like to contribute to my local village magazine - Over the Wall.

I had known Over the Wall for some time. Every few months I would hear the click of the letterbox and there on the doormat would be another crisp white copy. As well as the usual items on gardening, you could find tips on the care of guinea pigs, reports on the latest meeting of the parish council and accounts of the *good old days* when there were no fewer than 7 pubs in the village and regular fights at closing time. And now, to be invited to contribute - *and only 18 years after first moving to the village* - I had to pinch myself to check I wasn't dreaming.

The editor explained that he had an idea for a new column - something along the lines of *The Village Idiot* - and that he thought I would be just the man to write it. I must confess I was flattered. All the same, I wasn't too sure about the village idiot bit. I mean, it's not the most sensitive term and, besides, I had a feeling the position might be filled already. The last thing I wanted to do was to go muscling in on someone else's territory. So as an alternative, I came up with what I considered to be a far superior proposition -- namely a column concerned with reflections on the human condition and the nature of existence, drawn from my extensive experience of the world. The editor said that this sounded just perfect - and maybe he hadn't explained himself well enough -

but it was *exactly* what he had been trying to describe in the first place. He's a strange man and I have to say, I don't always follow his reasoning.

It only remained for me to decide upon a *nom de plume* and, after a little thought, I opted for *Wormwood*. Besides having a pleasantly Dickensian ring to it, the name contained a subtle clue to my own place of residence which, while thwarting the vulgar attentions of the riffraff, would permit people of *superior intelligence* to decipher my identity.

This is how it all began; this is how there came to be a *Wormwood* in *every single edition* of Over The Wall for the next ten years.

Till recently these pearls have been the exclusive preserve of a small Gloucestershire village on the edge of the Cotswolds. Now, via the medium of Mr Bezos's *Electronic Book*, they can be enjoyed by the entire world.


Horsley,
December, 2012

# Our expanding village

The fact that you are reading this means it is very likely you are a resident of Horsley[1]. And if you are one of those who has opted to forgo the soft-living of the village centre in favour of a wild and precarious existence on the parish margins, you'll know from first-hand experience what a very big place our village is.

Though Horsley is unlikely ever to have been an *ordinary* sort of village, it was not always the monster it is now. Quite how or when it attained its present immense size is unknown but there is evidence to suggest that there were long periods of stability punctuated by sudden spurts of explosive growth. During the most dramatic of these, the adjoining town of Nailsworth was swallowed up in the course of a single October night – a fact that Nailsworth residents have still not wholly taken on board.

Now there are indications that the village is stirring once again. Mysterious signs and portents abound: a doubling in the number of bagpipe permits issued by Pinfarthing post office; the miraculous birth of a pantomime-ready, Velcro™ foal at Folly Bank Farm and news that organisers of this year's annual walk around the parish boundary have found it necessary to include an overnight stop.

Viewed in isolation, any one of these might be dismissed as a simple oddity. Taken together however

---

[1] Of course, in the light of Wormwood's new-found international fame, this is no longer strictly true.

they point to an inescapable and disturbing conclusion. After a long period of slumber, Horsley is once again on the move.

Quite where it will end is anybody's guess, but one thing is for sure, the maps will need to be redrawn. Mark my word – they'll have the theodolites out any day now. See if I'm not right.

# Horsley uncovered

It is common knowledge that our village is riddled with tunnels. As well as the legendary tunnel connecting Horsley Court with the Priory (down which despairing prisoners were dragged to face trial before the notorious Judge Jefferies and his Bloody Assize), there are many more – some so tiny as to require the explorer to crawl on hands and knees, others large enough to admit horse and rider, two abreast.

Some of the tunnels lead quite a long way. One of my favourites starts underneath the refrigerated display in the village shop and runs all the way down to the rectory before descending steeply to Washpool. This last section entails a long, hazardous descent down countless slippery, stone steps, wetter and wetter all the while until, somewhere just beyond the Washpool itself, the tunnel comes to a seeming dead-end.

I confess, the first time I discovered this I was utterly flummoxed, but on closer examination it was apparent that the roof of the passageway incorporated some kind of moveable panel.

Imagine my surprise when, on pushing the panel aside, I emerged head and shoulders inside one of the Wilkins' kitchen cupboards! I knew it was them because I could overhear them arguing.

In the end, it took all my powers of self-control to resist the temptation to fling open the cupboard door and say: 'Boo!'

It would have been worth it just to see the look on their faces.

# The pageant of nature

At this time of year we are accustomed to bid farewell to our friends from the animal kingdom who have graced our hills and wooded valleys throughout the long summer months. And of all the species, it is the humble dappled duck that evokes the strongest emotions. This little bird - so plain and inconspicuous in ones and twos - when massing for its autumn migration above the misty autumn woods, presents a spectacle which, once witnessed, will be forever etched on the memory.

Even while our eyes are drawn to the skies, that old friend, the blue marmot (*arctomys azurus*) is preparing his winter bed. In former times a midwinter meal of roasted marmot was frequently all that stood between survival and slow starvation. And yet, nowadays there are few who can even *begin* to discover his hiding place.

And as the nights grow longer, it is time once again to go to the garage or cellar and get out your toad nets. Though it is rarely earlier than mid-November that the projectile toad (*bufo ballisticus*) adopts its challenging seasonal behaviour, those of you with young children and expensive garden furniture will want to be well-prepared.

We are blessed, in Horsley, with an almost unique diversity of nature's precious bounty; and yet even here we are not spared the slow decline of species and habitats.

Older members of the parish will recall the startling

annual bloom of the meadow narcissus, that for just one night of the year would paint every field in pulsating, iridescent hues; or the feathered newt (*triturus pennatus*) - once commonplace and now so rarely seen.

We may pride ourselves on hosting a healthy colony of the bashful vole (*microtus vercundus*) but alas, as for the meadow narcissus and the feathered newt, we will never see their like again.

# Thinking big

Now that every little hamlet has its donkey, isn't it time to raise the stakes and foster a truly magnificent animal – a veritable lord of beasts. We should get an elephant. We should have a Washpool[1] elephant.

Yes, I know – it's amazing isn't it; the rightness of the idea, once you *see* it. You wonder how it is we didn't think of it before.

Whether decorated and garlanded on festive days or trumpeting distantly on moonlit nights, the Washpool elephant will be a joy and a comfort to us all. And with duties so light as to be almost unnoticeable – shifting logs, washing cars, transporting children to and from school – it will live a life of fulfilment and variety, loved and venerated by the entire community.

Of course, there are the winters to think of; but we'll make it a house on the patch of grass just opposite the washpool – a suitably sturdy, oak-framed affair with a cosy thatched roof and a plentiful supply of fragrant hay. And on autumn nights, as the bonfire catches hold and friendly faces are touched by its glow, off to one side, beyond the first circle of firelight, a broad and ancient forehead might be seen – or sensed rather – swaying gently, in the doorway of its massive hutch.

Like little children, we venture forward to peer into the shadows, halted and mesmerised by the dull gleam of firelight on silver tusk ornaments, and wreathed, all

---

[1] One of the Horsley hamlets – named for a pool used to wash sheep.

the while, in coils of frosty breath - smelling of pesto sauce.

We should get one – I'm serious.

# Nympsfield

Out to the west, beyond the setting sun, lies the semi-mythical village of Nympsfield[1].

Despite the fact that Nympsfield is our nearest neighbour, very few Horsley villagers have ever been there and, of these, even fewer can honestly recount more than the merest outlines of their experience beyond a vague recollection of forced participation in obscure rituals. It is as if a mysterious field of forgetfulness overtakes the visitor shortly after taking one of those strange turn-offs into the village.

I went there myself last year, fully aware of the village's reputation and armed with a digital video camera with which I hoped to capture an objective record of the experience. Needless to say, on playing back the tape, there was nothing but useless static.

The expedition was not entirely fruitless however. On carefully examining the track of my GPS recorder, I discovered a remarkable fact. Nympsfield is a village in which *there are only right-hand turns*. I am now engaged day and night in trying to understand the laws that might explain this phenomenon.

In the meantime, I am interested in interviewing candidates for a new expedition scheduled for next month. If you are fit, pure in body and mind and immune to the enticements of the flesh please feel free to apply.

---

[1] Horsley's nearest neighbour

# Cultural diversity

Sociologists and other such types are very fond of saying how wonderful it is to have diverse communities, in which people of different back-grounds, beliefs and philosophies all live together in an atmosphere of harmony and mutual respect.

Well that's all very nice on paper, but here in Horsley we're experts at this sort of thing and we know a thing or two when it comes to cultural diversity. The startling fact is that in this small village there are almost as many different sub-cultures as there are households.

And what is more, it doesn't matter whether you're a silver-haired poet, evil scientist, philosopher, quack-therapist, SUV driver, hunt-follower, tree-hugger or wicked woodsman: the truth is, your neighbours are likely to be unanimous in agreeing you're a bit of a prat.

In case this seems unnecessarily depressing, just bear in mind that there are plenty of people with whom you can share similar prejudices about everyone else and this will more than make up for any feelings of isolation. Shameful though it might seem at first, this is the true cement that binds our community.

If you are still sceptical, consider right now how you're thinking:

'Just who is this Wormwood character anyway? Does he imagine that he's making me laugh? Because, if that's the case, I've got news for him.'

And then picture to yourself all the other readers of

Over the Wall who are thinking exactly the same thoughts.

There, you see - you're feeling better already.

# Cat litter

If there is a hell, I like to think there is a special section reserved for those people who run junk mail competitions – you know, the ones that say:

'Congratulations, you have already been selected for our £20,000 prize.'

An elderly aunt of mine fell victim to these people and used to send them nearly all her pension, often accompanied by touching little notes expressing her pleasure and excitement at the imminent windfall – which, of course, never materialised. Instead, each new day simply brought a further immense load of fancy envelopes, containing cleverly-crafted deceptions and empty promises.

I tried reasoning with my aunt; I tried to get her to see that she was being taken advantage of, but she had an instant retort — explaining how she was reliant on the high-volume of incoming mail for making cat-litter which she produced, one or two sacks-full daily, with a hand-cranked shredder. Indeed, by the time she died her cat-litter operation had attained near-industrial proportions. She would sit patiently at her table, turning the handle and feeding in all of the envelopes and the letters from the many competitions she 'didn't follow' - as she put it. What she really meant was that she had only enough blood in her veins for three or four competition organisers to feast on at a time and the others would just have to wait their turn.

When she died – my dear, infuriating, stubborn old aunt, who worked all her life in a washing machine factory, wrote poetry and painted watercolours - my one consolation was that, as a source of nourishment to her exploiters, she was entirely used up.

# Workaholics anonymous

Make no mistake, living with a workaholic is something that will test you to the limit.

I know, because it is my daily reality.

Most of the time, workaholics don't appear any different from normal people. It's just that, while most people can go out, do a bit of work and then come home again, for the workaholic this is the time when the really serious stuff begins.

I tried talking with her about it one morning, just before Christmas. I told her I didn't mind the long hours but I wanted her to bring it under some sort of control – say three nights a week at first and then, after a while, to try a whole weekend. She must have realised her problem had been getting out of hand because she agreed to give it a go.

For a while, everything seemed wonderful and we found ourselves doing those little things we'd done earlier in our marriage - watching Emmerdale together or passing-out over a bottle of vodka. But I secretly knew it was too good to last. The signs were there; I just didn't want to see them.

It was when I found used post-its at the bottom of the bedclothes that the time had come to stop pretending. I confronted her with them but she denied all knowledge and said she'd never seen them before. I think it was the lies that hurt me the most. So I decided to get devious myself and while she was out one day I searched the house from top to bottom. What I discovered made me realise just how serious her problem had become.

Hidden at the back of the drinks cupboard, there was a jar full of pens - not just regular biros, but fancy rollerballs and several colours of highlighter – while the drawer under the bed, which at first sight contained nothing more than an innocent collection of exotic lingerie, handcuffs and sex-toys, had a false bottom concealing an entire stationery cupboard - staplers, ink cartridges and blocks of post-its - still in their cellophane wrapping.

It was then that I realised it was no use confronting her anymore; I had to learn to understand and to accept her for who she is.

And that is how we live now - facing each day as it comes.

# Wormwood's wonderful website

Nowadays it seems that just about everyone has 'a great idea for a web site'. It's pathetic. I mean to say - who do they think they're fooling?

Now Wormwood - on the other hand - has a 'truly great idea for a web site'. Brace yourselves, fellow villagers, to be the first to hear about:

www.itsthethoughtthatcounts.com

As a client of this bold and truly unique enterprise, you simply register (for a small fee) the names, addresses and dates of birth of your dearest friends and relatives, together with a short psychological profile of each. And, having done that, you just sit back and leave everything else to us.

We will commit to sending greeting cards and gifts, on your behalf, to all registered individuals at appropriate times throughout the year.

No more worries about missing the birthdays of obscure nephews. Banished, the purgatory of the Christmas card list. Gone, the fear of waking up in a cold sweat with the realisation that you have overlooked your own 10th wedding anniversary. We at www.itsthethoughtthatcounts.com will look after everything.

All cards will bear a personal message written in a hand indistinguishable from your own. Gifts will be selected to delight or dismay the recipient, in accordance with your confidential wishes. We'll even forward you a picture of the ghastly tie you have just 'sent' to your Uncle Norman.

When it comes to Christmas cards, why not surprise your friends with that hand-made, ('Oh my God, how do they find the time?') look. Courtesy of our affiliates in the Philippines, we offer two separate styles at very reasonable rates:

Option 1:   Infant school *pathetic*. Glued pasta and glitter

Option 2:   *Sensitive, enigmatic*. Frayed linen, dried leaves, etc.

A modest additional monthly charge will bring you the benefits of our five-star service, including:

- Flowers seemingly personally delivered (inexpertly wrapped, left on doorstep in the rain)

- Other people's wedding anniversaries (NOTE: customers will be required to undergo a short counselling session prior to selecting this option)

- Gifts incorporating references to shared experiences: ('How well I recall the wonderful spring we spent together in Budapest!')

- Valentine cards with authentic 'tell-tale' postmark.

- Easter bunny service.

Of course, it might all come horribly unstuck - but hopefully, by that time, I will be well away.

# Slugs – a fortune at our feet

Never one to pass up the prospect of fame and fortune, Wormwood has been investigating an unlikely source of nature's bounty – slugs and snails.

I hear shouts of 'Why not include puppy dogs' tails, while you're at it?'

To which I can only reply: 'Don't be ridiculous. If you're not going to take this seriously I'll stop right now.'

No – the first inkling of this vast untapped economic resource first occurred to me while walking in the mountains of Northern Spain. At a certain point in my route, while passing through a sheltered valley, I noticed the path was alive with enormous slugs – the colour and size of bananas.

'If one were to harvest these', I thought, 'you could slice them thinly and flash fry them in olive oil. They would make a delicious, organic alternative to crisps.'

What to call them – that was the main problem. A friend ventured the suggestion: *Nature Bites* and it seemed nothing could stand in the way of astounding success. But fate was to snatch good fortune from my grasp; I could never find my way back to that valley. Despite wandering the mountain passes for months on end, my quest was to prove hopeless.

Back home once again, I found myself pondering the potential of our common or garden slug, but it was no use. However hard I tried to persuade myself, they were too small to make the kind of snack I had in mind.

I had been toying absentmindedly with 2 or 3 larger

specimens and was washing my hands when the thought struck me:

'This stuff must be more slippery than just about anything else in the world and what's more – *it takes some getting off.*'

What better illustration of how, in the presence of genius, the dull commonplace can be transformed – as if by magic – into shining inspiration.

Slug slime is the *perfect* lubricant. Initial trials have proved extremely promising and I even have a name for the final product – *Glide*.

The way it works is ....

**Ed:** As Wormwood has exceeded his word limit, I have been forced to cut the remainder of his article. This will undoubtedly come as a relief to many readers.

# Poste restante

At the age of 19 – like every other self-respecting hippy – I set out to hitch hike to The East. As phone calls were out of the question, my mother made me promise to send her the occasional postcard. She, in turn, wrote me a letter from home addressed: Poste Restante, Istanbul.

Trouble was - I never got it. After 3 weeks, I had reached the Bulgarian border and, tired and out of money, I turned round and headed back home.

And meanwhile, my mother's letter must have sat in some dusty old drawer in the Istanbul Head Post Office because 5 years later it came back – marked in blue pencil, in an unrecognisable language – stating: *Returned to Sender* or words to that effect in Turkish and covered in strange and mysterious stampings.

In these days of electronic communication, the fact that, for a modest amount of money, you can have a small physical object carried to the other end of the world – well I think it's nothing short of a miracle.

So I am busy writing myself letters and sending them off to the four-corners of the globe:

William Wormwood Esquire,
Poste Restante,
Aracataca,
Columbia;

ditto Buynaksk, Dagestan;
ditto Musselshell, Montana.

Call me a silly old fool but these late autumn evenings I like to gaze into the fire and imagine where my letters might have got to. Are they lying in a smelly sack in the corner of a depressing Central Asian warehouse, riding an Arctic Ocean swell or torn up and thrown away – filleted, in the expectation of finding money?

And if, by some miracle, they make it all the way to their destination – what then?

Picture the scene: an Alaskan settlement, a tiny general store. The door opens and a young but solidly built woman stumbles in, amidst a flurry of snow-flakes. She stamps her feet on the sodden cardboard that carpets the floor and pushes back the hood of her parka. Across the counter she catches the store-keeper's eye, asking the, by now, unspoken question:

*'So - any sign of that Wormwood guy?'*.

A slow raising of the head and a brief closing of the eyes is the only response from the old man behind the counter.

# Confessions of a commuter

When driving through a narrow village street, it's a good idea to tuck yourself in behind a truck. The truck goes blasting through the traffic and you follow on behind it. Time to listen to *In Our Time*, time to pick your nose.

But the truck goes straight on and you want to turn left. And suddenly you're face-to-face with another car at the end of a narrow street - half of it occupied by parked vehicles. He flashes you, even though he has right of way, and a wave of human gratitude brims over in your heart. Surging forward in acknow-ledgment, you give a small, ever so discreet, flash on the headlights as you swoop back into the left carriageway ...

**Ed:** Excuse me, but where exactly are we going with this?

It's my latest serial – Confessions of a Commuter – number 1 of 32 parts.

**Ed:** So how long till we get to the good bits ?

You mean, the bit where I graciously hold back whilst turning right so as to allow at least three lots of cars to come out in front of me ?

**Ed:** errr ...

So - if you'll allow me to continue:

And then, suddenly, here we are, nearly at the junction. I slow down at the roundabout, expecting it to be clear but –

Damn! Something coming. Stop!

I hate that feeling of having to stop, of having to get the car moving again. It seems so tortuous, so wasteful of precious energy.

But I leave these thoughts far behind as, accelerating down the slip road, I glide effortlessly onto the motorway, to take my rightful place in the middle lane.

And it is now that I surrender myself to reverie, to fantasies of escape, to the  compulsion to miss my exit, to thoughts of heading south - maybe all the way to Taunton ...

**Ed:** Can we have a talk ?

# WCOS

I've been reading in the papers about this carbon offsetting business.

It works like this. Say you want to fly by jumbo jet to New Zealand for your summer holidays (something which obviously none of us would even consider doing - but let's just imagine for a moment that you feel the compulsion to entertain such a shameful idea) then, on top of your air fare, you pay someone to plant about 15,000 oak trees. Over the next 50 years the trees will patiently soak up the carbon dioxide you are about to squander on your antipodean adventure, with the result that you can enjoy your holiday in the reassuring knowledge that you are 'on the side of the planet'.

Apparently this is big business all of a sudden. So, never one to be left behind when it comes to cutting-edge ideas, I have been giving the matter serious thought and, after a number of tough meetings with business types, venture capitalists and the like, I am proud to announce:

## The Wormwood Carbon Offsetting Scheme.

We're not planting any trees though; we've got far too many around here already. No, our idea – in a manner that seasoned readers will recognise as character-istically brilliant – goes straight to the heart of the matter.

Whatever the bewildering variety of complicated ways in which we generate greenhouse gases (threatening the delicate balance of life and so on) they all boil down to this: we live lives that are simply too fast, too wasteful - volume turned up to 11, throttle wide open, needle on red etc.

Now at last there is a solution - and the good news is this: **there is no need to change your lifestyle**; no need to put on the hairshirt of environmental contrition, nor the heavy woollen stockings of ecological correctness.

No. Leave it to us; we at WCOS are experts in this sort of thing.

For a small fee, we will compensate for the wasteful and embarrassing excesses of your own lifestyle with carefully matched periods of indolence or discomfort undertaken by our team of professional associates.

By way of example: a cheap return flight to Lanzarote is offset, at our end, by 4 hours dozing in a hammock; for which the fee will be £50 – enabling you to come home, not just stress-free and with an impressive tan, but confident in the assurance that you are *Carbon Neutral*.

That summer evening barbecue, which might otherwise have been marred by torments of guilt, can be enjoyed with a completely clear conscience, safe in the knowledge that, for a modest outlay of £15, we have people willing to spend a night in the open, in a state bordering on hibernation.

So go ahead, turn up that patio heater - we have it covered.

# Sausages

It's only very rarely that you'll catch me reading the food pages. Today was one of those exceptions, as I found myself listlessly scanning the Guardian Weekend for ideas for this piece.

(I know it will come as a shock and a disappointment to many - but even genius can occasionally find itself in need of inspiration).

So you can imagine my surprise on reading that Horsley sausages have been pronounced *The Best in the World* (Matthew Fort, Guardian weekend, July 14 2007).

As a resident of Horsley of some years standing, my first response was one of immense pride. All the same – let's be realistic – it's a worrying development. Give it a week or two and there'll be all sorts of flash cars parked along The Street, queues out of the shop doorway and buyers from Fortnum and Mason round the back with mobile phones, snapping up whole batches of sausages as fast as they can make them.

We once visited a Scottish fishing port; and could we find fresh fish to eat? No way! It was down to the Fisherman's Mission for us, for fish fingers and chips.

So the best we can hope for is that it will all blow over after a month or two and we can get back to normal.

In the meantime, Wormwood has been exploring the remoter regions of the culinary arts and, in particular, the bizarre and, some might say, perverse practices grouped under the heading: *illusion foods*.

By way of illustration, at the wedding banquet of Elizabeth of Austria and Charles IX – the principal dish featured a knight in the form of a grilled capon (complete with paper helmet and lance), mounted on the back of a roast piglet.

Other examples include chocolate cabbages, false lampreys and mock hedgehogs – the latter, a sort of haggis decorated with slivered almonds.

On second thoughts - maybe I'll get myself down to Horsley village stores and place an advance order for the sausages.

# Killing machine

My neighbour has a cat called Maude. That's a nice name for a cat.

It brings to mind a picture of a cat asleep on a cushion – the kind of picture you find in a certain sort of children's book, the kind that makes them feel jolly lucky to be growing up in the Cotswolds.

Maybe there's a cosy fire in the background and a tray to one side with a chubby teapot, a wisp of steam curling from it's spout and, alongside – a stripey mug and a plate of buns. Oh yes, and the cat's got a little wavy line of zzzz's rising above it – signifying content-ed purrs.

But oh what horrors this homely picture belies. I have another name for my neighbour's cat - not Maude, but *Killing Machine*!

I recall, earlier in the year; I was sitting by the pond – my thoughts lulled to an intoxicated reverie by the gentle warmth of a perfect, English summer afternoon. A huge dragonfly buzzed across the surface of the water - an iridescent marvel; its abdomen banded in electric blue and black.

When - SNAP !!!

Killing Machine (who had been lurking nearby) made her move and seized the miraculous creature from the very air.

Crunch, crunch ...

I have to say: the sight of her obvious discomfort in

getting the wings down afforded a small – if ultimately distasteful – compensation.

It's not just dragonflies. Mice, shrews, birds of every species (barring the major raptors) and slow worms. The last I feel for particularly; bitten in half and left to writhe in separate pieces. But please don't imagine I have any grudge against Killing Machine. After all, they say: 'It's in their blood' and, yes, I believe it.

No – it's us! We're the ones to blame !

Imagine what our little village must look like to a vole.

To a vole, our village is a zone inhabited by shambling, two-legged giants – slow and generally good-natured but, nevertheless, with an odd inclination to nurture to their bosom unnaturally large numbers of one of the most efficient predators known to creation.

Believe me. To the voles, our village is a place of dread, a no-go area, a spine-chilling and terrifying killing field.

# Waste of space

I've lost count of the number of times I've attempted to sort through the stuff in my cellar.

It starts out well enough; here's an odd gardening glove, with a hole in the thumb. No question about it – straight into the bin. Dried up superglue – ditto. Dead batteries. Whatever was I thinking of hanging onto these – *clang*.

But wait a minute ...

What I was actually thinking was:

'best dispose of these responsibly.'

So maybe I should keep them until I have the time to find out what responsible disposal entails.

Did you see that? Did you notice that moment when my concentration falters?

From that point on, everything starts to go downhill.

It's not long before I find myself dithering over an enamel mug full of old CND badges ('surely these will be of great interest to future generations') or, even worse, a good quality padlock (locked) – minus key of course, but   '... I'm sure it must be around here somewhere – *I certainly wouldn't have thrown it away*.'

And subtly, imperceptibly, my activity switches from finding things to get rid of to one of sorting stuff into different containers.

Please tell me I'm not alone.

Actually, I know I'm not alone because I've heard of other people who have moved on to Stage 2.

Stage 2 being:
1. Give up trying to get rid of anything
2. Accept the inevitable.
3. Look into the best deals on self-storage.

Do you know, the British Library holds a copy of absolutely every single book and magazine published, simply because they *can't be arsed* to decide which ones are worth keeping - so they keep the lot. They're experts at stage 2; they know all about it.

For those of us without the luxury of an abandoned saltmine or disused aircraft hangar, Stage 2 represents a serious challenge. The fact is, the modern home is simply not up to the demands placed upon it by a mature consumer economy. There is nowhere near enough space to store the stuff we feel compelled to buy. My own advice is 'stop thinking cupboards - think attached warehouse'. Better still, 'think seriously large warehouse, with modest, attached living accommodation'.

I've heard it said that Stage 3 is where you pick up a small rucksack, quietly close the door behind you and take to the open road – but I'm not there quite yet.

## Community service

I've never been one to blow my own trumpet but I take great pride in the various little ways in which I try to contribute to the smooth running of our community. Take today for example - straight after breakfast it's straight down to Nailsworth bus station to help *see-off* the 8:47 to Gloucester.

Despite the fact that I have recently taken to using a pair of regulation fluorescent paddles (of the sort employed at airports) to assist in guiding the buses out, the drivers show a lamentable ignorance of even the most elementary marshalling signals. The driver this morning got quite worked up about it and I decided it was better to make a run for it.

It seemed a good time to pop into the supermarket to check on the shelf-stacking. Sadly, it took no more than the briefest visual inspection to confirm that much remains to be done in that department.

I don't know how many times I've had to explain it to the staff there, but when it comes to choosing a pot of yoghurt, customers prefer the ones with a long sell-by date, so placing these at the back of the shelf is most unhelpful.

I had just put all the yoghurts back in the right order and was moving on to do the same with the double cream when the manager appeared and got quite unnecessarily upset. I explained to him that it was a wholly understandable mistake, can't have eyes in the back of his head and so on. But privately, this isn't the first time I've had to correct this particular slip-up and

I am sure it must be embarassing for him to be repeatedly reminded of the fact.

Fortunately, at that moment, the situation was saved by the arrival of two police officers – and I remembered that it was at least a fortnight since I had given them one of my morale-boosting talks.

Back at the police station the lady officer made a very nice little speech of her own along the lines that, while she appreciated my public spiritedness, she INSISTED that I try to reduce my various duties and leave the work to others. I can't remember her precise words – but it was something along those lines.

For my part, I made it clear that for as long as chaos and inefficiency continue to plague the town they would not find me letting up – at which point the male police officer insisted that, on the contrary, I really MUST stop, otherwise he couldn't vouch for the consequences. The earnestness and sincerity with which they begged me not to overtax myself was altogether quite touching I thought.

So generally, despite the usual trivial frustrations - a wholly worthwhile and productive day, not to mention the ride home in a police car with my own driver – an honour that seemed wholly lost on Mrs Wormwood.

But then she's always the last one to appreciate my qualities.

## Summer ... or what

For my father, the thought of going on holiday any later than mid-July was out of the question. The way he saw it was that by August *they'd be pulling the boats up,* as he used to put it, or *storing away the deck chairs* -- or if not actually doing these things, they'd be starting to think about them - and that was just as bad.

No, the perfect fortnight for our Cornish seaside holiday was the last week in June, first week in July: when summer suddenly bursts out with exhilarating vitality and it seems quite reasonable to believe that the long midsummer days might last forever.

Mornings, cool and bright -- light sparkling on crystal-clear water; the evenings -- balmy, the harbourside aglow with yellow lamplight, set against a peaceful, turquoise sky.

Provided it wasn't raining, of course.

A rainy holiday was enough to plunge my father into bleak despair. Even the prediction of rain was enough to put the dampers on an otherwise perfect day.

'You enjoy it while you can', he would pronounce gloomily, as we lolled in the warm sunshine. 'I know what's coming.'

So, all in all, I think it best he was spared our recent summers.

For my own part, I have developed a technique for coping with the despondency brought on by the daily sight of rain falling from a featureless, leaden sky and that is to play the 'there's always someone worse off than I am' game.

I try thinking about what it must be like to be a farmer, a road-mender or one of those people inviting shoppers to fill in questionnaires, before it finally hits me that the person I would least like to be on a rainy day in July is the man selling donkey rides on the beach at Weston-Super-Mare.

Just picture the scene: a makeshift lean-to, hard against the sea wall – no floor, just bare sand, littered here and there with donkey-droppings. The donkey-man himself, slumped in a sagging picnic chair, leafs through a dog-eared copy of Take a Break – long past bothering even to glance across the deserted, windswept beach. And, all the while, a bunch of sodden donkeys, blunt heads lowered, steam patiently in the gloom.

You have to be careful though -- think about it too much and you can end up feeling even worse.

# Monopoly money

It has been clear to me for a long time that the game of Monopoly should come with a health warning along the lines: 'May give rise to sudden and uncontrollable acts of violence'. Certainly as a child, the closest I came to murdering anyone, was when playing Monopoly on the hearthrug with my little brother.

The following was a typical scenario. My brother would build up a massive sub-prime property portfolio based on the cheap streets on the first two edges of the board while I pursued an alternative strategy focusing on top-quality investments. Having secured both Park Lane and Mayfair and painstakingly built up to a hotel on each, I would patiently wait for my brother's token to land on one of the fateful squares. When it did, I would rub my hands together and start chuckling, in the confident knowledge his pathetic financial empire was doomed.

But then he would calmly reach beneath the edge of the hearthrug and pull out a thick bank-roll of red, £500 pound notes – which he'd been quietly squirreling away since the beginning of the game – and coolly pay off the debt as if it was of no consequence to him whatsoever.

He had a further trick or two up his sleeve when it came to real money too. For example, he would POLISH his pocket money. He'd work away at his pennies with Brasso™ until they shone like newly-minted gold sovereigns. At first, I considered this a faintly amusing, babyish aberration; but that was before he played his masterstroke.

When the tinkling notes of 'Popeye the Sailor Man' heralded the arrival of the ice-cream van, and we all rushed out with our pennies, my brother sat dejectedly on the doorstep in such a way as to catch the eye of our mother, who immediately asked him why he wasn't first in the queue for an ice-cream, whether he was feeling poorly etc.

'No.' he said – lifting sorrowful eyes in which I could swear he had managed to cause real tears to glisten. 'It's just that I don't want to spend all my shiny money.' At which point – and I found this scarcely credible in our mother, who was normally so canny – she gave him some extra money for an ice cream! I can still remember the little smile he saved just for me, as he joined the queue.

He runs a small music business these days.

Strange – he might have had a great career in banking.

# A dose of optimism

Someone once said that optimism is no longer optional - it's compulsory (things being so bad and all) and I have to say I couldn't agree more. These days we all have to make a special effort to brighten ourselves up and put on a cheery face - if only out of consideration for our friends.

If I'm out on the street - for example - and I spot a neighbour on the opposite pavement, I make a point of crossing the road to greet them in a jolly tone of voice, before stopping to chat for a few minutes about the state of the weather or to share an amusing story about a fellow villager. If it's a guy, I might give him a friendly dig in the ribs or a hearty slap on the back. It's not difficult; you just have to make a bit of an effort.

Wormwood: 'Is that enough?'

Ed: '... a bit more'

Wormwood: 'OK'

It was all so different in the old days; life was easier somehow.

In those days, you couldn't step out of your front door without finding yourself in a throng of happy people busily going about their business - eyes sparkling with vitality and the eager anticipation of whatever the day ahead might bring.

Or in the fields on a balmy summer evening, where mothers would bring their children to pick black-berries; the faces of the young women flushed with colour and crowned with golden locks - all alight in the late afternoon sun; while a little baby - watched by his sister - grasps at a passing butterfly before tottering gently forward into the warm grass.

Many's the evening we spent in the Old Bell and Castle; a half-circle of merry companions gathered around the log fire, faces aglow with happiness and wellbeing. Ah, the gales of laughter, the thighs slapped in mirthful abandon as some rascally old character had us all in stitches.

And then later, round the back with Mary in the moonlight - her soft ....

**Ed:** 'OK, that'll do.'

**Wormwood:** '... but I was just getting to the good bit.'

**Ed:** 'I know, but we'll have to leave it there'

**Wormwood:** 'Very well, but heaven knows whom we're disappointing'

# Natural gardening

As far as the garden is concerned, Mrs Wormwood and I are keen proponents of what is known as *The Natural Look*.

Let me stress right away however that the creation of a truly natural garden entails hours of research, planning and execution. Not everyone will have the time or interest to explore this highly-specialised activity.

Take the lawn for example. While most people content themselves with a flat, tightly-cropped surface comprising a single species such as a fine-bladed fescue, we opted instead for a distressed finish in which a rich diversity of grasses and small flowering plants are interspersed with patches of bare earth. Starting with a conventional lawn that, in essence, served as our blank canvas, transformation to the present mature state required patient attention over a period of several years.

A similar degree of care has been lavished on the boundary wall of our property which is just nearing completion and in which we have explored a different set of ideas. Here the underlying theme is a crumbling stone wall over which a delicate filigree of ivy, brambles and goosegrass has been skillfully woven into a single rich mat. The effect we were striving for and which, without undue modesty, I believe we can claim some success in achieving, is reminiscent of the paintings of the Pre-Raphaelites and in particular that great masterpiece of William Holman Hunt: Our

English Coasts.

As far as the beds are concerned, we really let ourselves go here - playing with the idea of paired plants, in which individuals of one variety are set-off against a denser companion that serves as a backdrop. Thus: foxgloves in a sea of nettles, comfrey bedded in ground elder and rose bay willow herb swaying gracefully over a cushion of chickweed.

As is the case with so many other areas of life, goals that are worth attaining don't come for free. To become a natural gardening expert calls for clarity of purpose and a willingness to let go of cherished patterns of behaviour.

'I think the idea sounds great' I hear you say, 'but I don't know how to take the first step.'

Well I've got great news for you and thousands more like you: the Wormwood Wildgarden Workshop (www.www.com) – an intensive, hands-on course that will teach you all you need to know about converting your own garden to the Natural Look.

Cost £50, Chairs provided. Bring a bottle.

# Football

As far as football is concerned, everything began to go wrong for me around the age of nine. We'd just started playing football at school and we had to provide our own boots.

While my friends all turned up in flashy black and white footwear – newly available in the shops and known as Continentals - my mum decided to buy me a good solid pair of brown leather boots of a style not dissimilar to a miner's boot with leather studs nailed on the bottom.

It was not very long before I became aware that my boots had a name. My boots – as my friends were quick to point out – were of a type known as *Old English*. Just the job for kicking over dustbins but distinctly limited when fancy footwork was called for.

For a while I was tolerated in the team for the knack I had of crippling the opposition. One nifty kick to the shins with my Old English was sufficient to bring the first-aid box out. But there was no getting away from it; from the day my mum bought me those boots my footballing days were doomed.

... worse than that; I failed somehow to develop into a normal, healthy football supporter.

Many is the time I've envied my football-supporting friends. For them every winter Saturday promises an evening of either ecstatic happiness or bleak despair depending on whether their team wins or loses – whereas for me, one Saturday is very much like the next.

Ask the football enthusiast to explain the meaning of life and you'll get a clear, concise and direct answer. Ask me the same question and I'd be forced to admit that I'm not absolutely sure. That's how bad it gets.

No, there's no arguing with the fact that the person who is indifferent to football is a figure to be pitied.

So mums (and dads), when you take your child to buy their first pair of football boots, buy them the Mizuna Morelia - hand-stitched from genuine kangaroo leather and endorsed by some of the world's top goal-scorers. They may cost as much as a weekend for two in Paris but it's a small price to pay for your child's psychological wellbeing.

# Energy draining devices

There's something wonderful about unpacking a brand-new gadget. It's to do with the fact that, right up to the moment when you unwrap the item from its innermost polythene bag it is *perfect*.

Whether I have just bought a new camera or an electric nose-hair trimmer, on opening the box, I like to go straight for the instruction manual and read it from cover to cover. Only then do I feel ready to release the item from its factory-sealed confinement.

So OK – I admit it – I have a small stamp collection and I arrange my CDs in alphabetical order. But don't worry - there are lots more like me. Though it has to be said: Mrs Wormwood is not one of them.

We bought a new washing machine recently. The makers, very considerately, supplied two sets of instructions. There's the 27-page set that explains how to clean the pump, descale the drawer recess and perform what is described as an *emergency emptying* and then there's the single page, laminated card called 'How to put a wash on'. So we both had something to read.

Even when we have intelligent, user-friendly appliances it will end up the same way.

We order a new toaster together. It arrives. We unpack it and plug it in. There are little lights that make a smiley face. I glance at Mrs Wormwood and she nods almost imperceptibly, prompting me to speak.

'So tell me about yourself.' I ask the toaster

To which it chirpily responds:

'Do you want:

(a) my complete technical details or

(b) just enough information for operation without either damaging me or injuring yourself?'

No. It's a nightmare.

I picture myself arriving home. The house is strangely quiet. Mrs. Wormwood in the kitchen, arms folded, angry expression:

Wormwood: '... what's wrong?'

Mrs W: 'I swore at the TV and it went into a sulk and now all the other machines have reset themselves in sympathy.'

Wormwood: 'Oh darling ... not again! You know how long it takes to coax them round again.'

Mrs W: (stamping and on the brink of tears): 'I know!'

# A terrible beauty

Our world is a place ablaze with a terrible beauty. From the sight of distant mountains, restless sea and towering clouds, to the teeming tapestry of life itself. Sparkling eddies ruffle the surface of rock pools scattering diamond points of light. Leaves angle themselves to the sun; while on the woodland floor a myriad tiny creatures hurry this way and that. Everything is on the move, everything is in a state of flux. Bees gather nectar; worms patiently burrow; swifts weave across the sky.

Life is a palace with ten trillion rooms of which we humans have but one ...

**Readers:** Excuse me but when do we get to have a laugh?

**Wormwood:** I can't promise anything this time round I'm afraid. Best talk to the editor if you want to complain. Now if you don't mind, maybe I can continue. This is top-quality stuff you're getting here.

**Readers:** Because if we're not going to get a laugh, we're off.

**Wormwood:** Suit yourself.

Of course, many are the unfortunate people whose daily existence is one of unremitting ugliness and flat, depressing uniformity - their brutish lives spent in an endless quest for cheap sensation.

I have often wondered how it is that I have been spared such a fate; why it is I am fortunate to be blessed with an ever-present sense of being surrounded by beautiful things, of being immersed in beautiful thoughts. While there is no simple answer, I am convinced that it is due in part to the fact that the sight that greets me each morning in the bathroom mirror is one of unalloyed loveliness.

Many are the occasions when Mrs Wormwood has been forced to barge me away from entranced contemplation of my own reflection so as to make space for her own humble toilette. But then who could be other than mesmerised by the perfectly propor-tioned face: the mouth – sensuous, yet with a touch of vulnerability; eyes like twin pools of wisdom; the kingly brow symbolising ...

Ed: [flicking Wormwood switch to off position]

'OK. Bag it! Next !!'

# The Wormwoods on holiday

Mrs Wormwood and I have just returned from our annual holiday on the continent and, while we had a thoroughly enjoyable time, it was the outward journey that sticks in my mind.

It all started rather wonderfully. We were waiting in the departure lounge - I was reading my newspaper and Mrs Wormwood was knitting - when we were thrilled to hear our names announced over the public address system:

> *'Would Mr and Mrs Wormwood please proceed immediately to gate 7 where ALL the other passengers are waiting to board the aeroplane.'*

I thought that rather fine – the fact that ALL the other passengers were waiting for us to board first. All the same, as we walked towards the gate I found myself speculating as to what had occasioned this special treatment. I could only imagine that it had something to do with the fact that, in contrast to other people - who looked like they were dressed ready for the beach - I had chosen to dress in a manner that befits an English gentleman: cream linen suit, panama hat and brogues. And so it was with a small glow of pride that, having arrived at the departure gate, I led Mrs Wormwood to the front of the queue, nodding affably to fellow passengers and doffing my hat to the ladies.

Our arrival seemed to cause some excitement and, in the general stampede to board the aeroplane, Mrs Wormwood and I were separated and forced to sit apart. She was placed next to a young woman and in no time at all they were chatting away like old friends. My companion, on the other hand, was a young man wearing earphones. Every time I asked him a question he had to take them out of his ears and put them back again. For the life of me, I couldn't understand why he didn't just leave them out altogether.

An announcement was made that luncheon was about to be served and, on asking to see the menu, I received the somewhat brusque response: 'Chicken or curry?' Being unused to this sort of treatment, I repeated my request to see the menu and, on getting the same response a second time, I got out of my seat and strode down the gangway, determined to complain to the captain regarding the rude behaviour of his catering staff.

Then the strangest thing happened. On finding the cabin door jammed, I was trying to ease it open with my shoulder when some of the other passengers, forcibly grabbed me and returned me to my seat where they proceeded to lash my arms to the armrests with headphone wires. I protested that I was sure the seat belt was more than adequate when it came to the rigours of landing but they would have none of it and said that 'it was for my own safety.'

And, to cap it all, we were personally escorted off the plane by armed men in uniform. I know that an Englishman still attracts a degree of respect in foreign parts but this was far more than I might have expected.

Before we left for our hotel, Mrs Wormwood had a surprisingly lengthy conversation with another uniformed official who leafed repeatedly through my passport while studying me through the glass partition of his office. I imagine he was admiring my impecc-able dress sense.

As I say, it was all very wonderful.

# Personal transformation

I have to confess, I have been worried about myself lately. Why, only this morning I was forced to give myself a severe talking-to on account of a general tendency to sloppiness that has been creeping in for some time now.

It's not like it's an isolated incident. Last Friday, for instance, I caught myself idly daydreaming and otherwise behaving in an indolent and unproductive manner. That occasion was made doubly serious by the violent and abusive reaction that alerting myself to the problem provoked.

Of course, to the outside observer there is nothing to suggest the mass of chaos and indiscipline that lurks beneath my seemingly confident exterior. Having the advantage of inside information however, I can confirm that things have been seriously adrift for quite a while. And, as neither reasoning nor reprimand appear to have had any effect, there was no alternative other than to read myself the Riot Act (as they say) and to give myself a thorough seeing-to.

Ah, the pleadings, the promises, the extravagant pledges and sobs of protest were pitiful to witness. But I remained stern and unmoving. If the drift toward degeneracy and laziness is to be halted and, hopefully one day, reversed there is nothing else for it than to subject myself to a strict daily regime:

9am. The day starts with consciousness-raising exercises in the form of an unhurried emergence from sleep. Fulfilment of normal bathroom functions is followed by a breakfast of coffee and croissants. Physical exercise in the form of a casual stroll though the woods completes the first component.

The second half of the morning is devoted to the development of motor functions, reactions and mental dexterity. After much experimentation, I have found both Lara Croft, Guardian of Light and Call of Duty, Modern Warfare II to be highly effective in this department. An intense session with either game is usually sufficient to round off the morning.

A light lunch is followed by a cultural programme, taking up the first part of the afternoon. A wide variety of material is covered ranging from the Marx Brothers to Quentin Tarantino but, in all cases, the mental effort is such as to necessitate a period of recuperation in the form of a short, 30-minute nap.

The next element is designed to exercise those faculties concerned with Politics and Social Engagement. It is more than adequately fulfilled by logging onto Twitter or Facebook for an hour or two and ranting on about the X Factor or Strictly Come Dancing.

The program continues right through to 6pm and beyond – being dedicated to decision-making skills: red or white, for example or, if that becomes too easy, in or out, top or bottom. That kind of thing.

No, there is no doubt about it; there are few things in life that can be attained without an element of self-discipline.

I am reconciled to that now.

# Quality of Life

The way I see it - it's like this:

We all have this thing called a *Standard of Living*. Some people have a high *Standard of Living*, others have to make do with something more modest. But whatever the size of your own *Standard of Living*, you can think of it as being made up of a lot of separate parts - each making a small contribution to the total score.

Now if you leave out the bits that are to do with your income, bank balance, size of house, fondness for champagne or tendency to fly off to the Caribbean then what you're left with is something called *Quality of Life*.

*Quality of Life* was invented a while back with the intention of giving everyone a sporting chance of winning every now and again. So, for example, if you are in good health, have food on the table and have friends or family around then you're in with a definite chance - provided of course that the game is being played according to *Quality of Life* rules.

The problem with playing according to the *Standard of Living* rules was that the same people kept winning time and time again and it was beginning to look like the game was rigged.  So nowadays there's broad agreement that *Quality of Life* is the one to go for even though it's obvious that quite a few people are playing *Standard of Living* at the same time – as a sort of side bet.

**Ed:** But hang on a minute. What's all this stuff about a game?

**Wormwood:** The *Game of Life*, of course. Is there another?  Now, if you don't mind; you're making me lose my train of thought.

**Ed:** Sorry.

What we're talking about here is the ordinary, standard-grade *Quality of Life*. Though authentic and perfectly enjoyable, it's fairly commonplace. There's a superior variety – what you might think of as pure, 24-carat *Quality of Life* – that is much more rare.

To find out whether you have any of this you just have to carry on leaving things out. So, as well as not counting material wealth, you're not allowed to score any points either for your social life, children, pets, hobbies, personal relationships, comfort and dignity in old age or even for being in a good state of health.

It's quite normal, at this point, for people to finish up with nothing at all. For a fortunate few however there is something left over, like a tiny flake of gold at the bottom of the pan.

If you could bottle it, you'd be a millionaire.

# Normal wisdom

I am frequently asked to explain what it is like to be a genius. Setting modesty aside, I can only say that for me it feels quite ordinary.

Many are the occasions when I find myself reeling back in amazement at my own accomplishments. Why only the other day, I had just finished cleaning some paint brushes when I was astounded to discover I had accidentally produced an abstract masterpiece, virtually indistinguishable from one of the better paintings by Jackson Pollock.

And when it comes to philosophy, it's much the same story. I've lost count of the times I have had insights into the big questions such as the nature of reality, the purpose of our life on earth and so on – insights that are of such startling clarity as to be quite literally inexpressible.

But I am not one to evade the responsibility that is the inevitable lot of those blessed with great intellect. Many are the occasions I have felt duty bound to communicate with academics and scientists either to highlight flaws in their research or to share points of detail designed to set them on the right path.

Only recently I had to correct a Nobel prize-winning physicist over a quite unjustified assertion he had made concerning the structure of sub-atomic particles. On another occasion, I considered I would have been failing in my duty as a citizen not to alert the guys at GCHQ to a subtle loophole in the mathematics underpinning their military encryption standards.

I can well understand why the GCHQ people didn't acknowledge my email. No doubt there are considerations of National Security to be taken account of, and besides, it would have been embarrassing for them to own up to such a blunder. But the lack of response from other quarters is less excusable. My suspicion is that the people with whom I have been generous enough to share my scientific insights are quietly squirreling them away, with the intention of passing them off as their own, later on.

No, there's no getting away from it: genius is a heavy burden and those who bear it must accustom themselves to treading a lonely road with scant acclaim from the common herd.

So it will come as no surprise to hear that after a day spent soaring amongst the rarefied heights of the intellect there is nothing I enjoy more than a quiet evening over a game of chess or backgammon with Mrs Wormwood.

I always let her win of course – it gives her such pleasure.

# Reality exposed

Throughout the dull, depressing days leading up to Spring I've been keeping myself busy dreaming up ideas for reality TV shows.

To be honest, I've very little time for reality TV; it really doesn't interest me. But I'm told the masses just lap it up - so who am I to disappoint them? And though the genre is weighed down with second-rate variations on the theme of food preparation - is it entirely beyond redemption? Might it not be revitalised by an injection of pure creative genius?

So .... the first idea is called **Bus Pass Safari**.

I can just see the tweets:

> *'Did you see Bus Pass Safari last night? Best thing I've seen this year! #BPS'*

Two teams of old people have to travel from (say) Colchester to Runcorn, equipped only with a duffel-bag full of sandwiches, a book of accommodation vouchers and a bus pass. There's surely no need to go into details; you can imagine the rest.

Then there's **Hobby Swap**. Train-spotting and karate; cake decoration and motorcycle scrambling. Hilarious.

But my best idea without a doubt is (I haven't quite decided on a name for it yet) - **Exposed** maybe, or **Can Run, But Can't Hide**.

In this one, a volunteer (and fortunately there's never any shortage of volunteers) is placed, naked, in a sealed, soundproof cylinder, transported to *this week's surprise location* and ... released.

Points awarded for creativity, poise and laughs (obviously).

Of course, the key to success lies in the choice of location:

- Stalls at the Royal Opera House, Covent Garden

- Millwall football club home ground - The Den (Cold Blow Lane End)

- Parade Ring, Crufts Dog Show

I appreciate it might not be to everyone's taste but there's no beating it for sheer elegance of concept.

# Pet hates

The first thing to say about 'pet hates' is that we don't just *have* them, we *nurture* them and it is this that lends the whole topic a shameful, slightly squalid quality. In fact, I can honestly state that I don't believe I have any pet hates – at least not in the sense of secret, obsessive loathings dwelt on in private. That said, as I go about my daily round, there are enough minor irritations, animosities and aversions to make up quite a decent list. So here they are - in no particular order:

- Liquorice Allsorts – all of them, but especially the ones with a coloured, gritty coating
- Bull bars on 4-wheel drives (might as well mount a 2ft steel spike on the front and be done with it)
- Rats
- Organisers of fake competitions – you know the ones that say: 'Congratulations, you have already been selected for our £25,000 jackpot'. These people should be marooned together (with no food) on a small desert island.
- People with a sense of superiority – as if wealth and good fortune were the outward mani-festations of inner qualities and not simply down to a series of lucky breaks.
- Assaults on public servants: nurses, traffic wardens, postal workers, bus-drivers etc.
- People who, on being offered chocolates/fancy cakes/luxury confections etc, declare that they never eat such things before going on to scoff the lot.

- Christmas round-robin letters – as if I actually give a *damn* about Henry's winning goal in the under-12's football final.
- Use of the phrase '*My other half*'. Suggesting that one considers oneself incomplete.
- Use of the phrase '*My better half*'. As above but with the addition of false modesty.
- Coconut pyramids
- **WILD WEST** style typefaces.
- Use of the phrase '*He/she was not one to suffer fools gladly*'. Implying that the person in question was quite prepared to suffer fools - but only begrudgingly.
- The term 'fine *toothcomb*' which brings to mind an implement for 'combing' the teeth and which – being fine – is made out of ivory and silver or suchlike. Surely what is meant is a fine-toothed *comb* – or am I missing something here?
- Use of the phrase '*little man*' as in 'I have a wonderful little man to clean my windows'
- Acapella music – and especially the eager expressions on the faces of the singers that imply the audience can't possibly be experiencing anything less than ecstatic rapture.
- Use of the phrase '*Going forward*' as in 'We anticipate further, sustained enhancement of our international financial standing - *going forward*'.
- Scottish bagpipes
- Ground elder
- Certain kinds of dog

Well that's about it. Goodness knows how many people I have managed to offend here.

# Dreams beyond your wildest dreams

Are you tired of having second-rate dreams? Do your dreams amount to no more than a slightly weird version of your normal working day? Do you pretend to have forgotten your dreams for fear you might be thought shallow and boring?

If this describes your dream life, then we have good news for you. For a modest outlay we can supply you with the dreams you never dared believe could be yours. Here is just a small sample of the products we have on offer:

**Fly like an Eagle**. Starting out in a treetop or at the top of a high building, you experience a fleeting moment of terror as you lose your balance only to discover that *you can fly*. We offer individual flight (eagle, heron, buzzard) as well as our highly-popular formation options (swift, starling etc).

**King of the World**: Rising from your bed on what at first appears to be an ordinary morning, you discover that you have won/inherited 10 million pounds. The rest of the dream is spent in excited anticipation of all the things that are suddenly possible. This is an unsophisticated yet highly effective product offered at a budget price. Customers are strongly recommended to follow it up with a second purchase such as *Fly like an Eagle* or *Opium Eater*, as otherwise the come-down on waking-up to the reality of your drab and uninteresting life can be quite severe.

**Dirty weekend**: An almost unlimited choice of partners and locations (campervan, beach-hut, country cottage, luxury hotel) will permit you to create a unique and utterly unforgettable experience. For our male customers we can offer Angelina Jolie, Cate Blanchett, Monica Bellucci and many, many more. For the ladies there's George Clooney (10% surcharge), Johnny Depp and Viggo Mortensen. Reductions available if opting for one's real-life partner.

**The Real Thing** (our premium product): Usually purchased as a romantic prelude to *Dirty Weekend*, this will allow you to enjoy the experience of falling in love in all its delightful and intoxicating intensity. For example, you are at Stroud Farmers market when you suddenly find yourself chatting to Miss Scarlett Johansson and it is immediately apparent that you are both irresistibly attracted to one another. Over coffee at a street-corner café, you discover there is so much more you want to share ...

**Opium Eater**: Transported by flying carpet to the palaces of the Orient, you feast your eyes on jewelled elephants, elaborate architecture and veiled dancing girls to the accompaniment of melodious gongs. In common with many of our products the sense of wellbeing persists long after waking. For this reason we recommend *Opium Eater* as a follow-up dream to *King of the World*, *The Real Thing* etc.

**Rock Star**: To the strains of 'Anthem for the Common Man' you find yourself taking to the stage in front of a crowd of 500,000 adoring fans. Customers should not confuse this with inferior products from rival companies in which stage-fright or the sudden realisation that you are stark naked can transform the whole experience into a nightmare. Be assured, this is the real thing.

All major credit cards accepted. Full catalogue available on request. Please note that product descriptions are provided for illustrative purposes only. Accuracy of dreams cannot be guaranteed. Proof of age required for certain products. We regret we cannot offer refunds in the event that the transition from The Real Thing to Dirty Weekend is interrupted by the intrusion of drinking buddies, sudden compulsion to explore your childhood home, streets turning into an ever-expanding maze of tiny alleyways and so on.

# On reflection

This time round I will be reflecting on ... Reflection.

And before you start, I should point out that this isn't my idea. We're actually set these topics you know. Last time it was *Dreams* and the time before that *Pet Hates*. (It's quite possible you hadn't noticed).

To be fair, The Man says we can write about anything we like and that the themes he comes up with are simply intended to be helpful. All the same, I wish he wouldn't do it. Once I've had the topic dangled in front of my nose I'm like a dog thrown a stick. I just can't resist chasing it.

But *Reflection* - I have to confess: this one's got me completely stumped; which is strange, as reflecting on things - in the sense of day-dreaming, wool-gathering and so on - is something I'm rather good at. I'm so good at it, in fact, that I assume it's entirely normal to spend two or three hours of every day, gazing empty-headedly at nothing in particular.

But wait a minute, I have an idea: what if I were to confront the challenge head on? If, just briefly, I were to draw back the curtain, revealing the exquisitely balanced machinery humming away at the core of the creative mind? Wouldn't that be something of a special treat for the readers?

Whatever. Here goes anyway. Brace yourselves:

Oh dear, it's twenty to midnight and 3 days past the deadline.

There's not much Christmas cake left. Maybe I'll have just a little bit.

You know, there's been a Wormwood in Over The Wall since day one[1].

I want a cup of tea.

What was that joke?

> They laughed when I told them I wanted to be a comedian. They're not laughing now.

All the same, I can't see them laughing at this one.

Well I didn't get much done today. Maybe tomorrow will be better.

Kettle boiled ages ago; I'll have to put it on again.

When someone is described as a 'bit of a philosopher' it usually means they can be found down the pub, propping up the bar and treating their fellow drinkers to a sluggish stream of nonsense.

There's that half-dead bluebottle again.

The Oxford English Dictionary (20 volumes. Oxford University Press, £750, but available online, for free, using your public library borrower number) states that the word 'bullshit' was first coined in 1915.

Will that do, I wonder?

The creative mind at work. Awesome - wouldn't you say?

All the same, I don't imagine it's something you want to see every day.

---

[1] On second thoughts, this is not quite true.

# A walk of two halves

Wormwood is in the middle of a long walk from Land's End to Cape Wrath, at the northwest tip of Scotland. He has posted this update on his progress - written 'on the hoof'.

It was on a long, lonely road in Shropshire that I came to the startling realisation that there are two of us doing this journey.

There's 'the bottom half' - the bit that does all the walking, negotiates fallen trees and climbs over stiles. Then there's 'the top half' - the part that gazes across distant vistas, lost in poetic reverie and philosophic reflection.

Needless to say, it is the top half that is writing this piece. It has been clear for quite some time that philosophic reflection is not one of the bottom half's strong points. The bottom half is not a great communicator. His conversation - if you can call it that - is confined to an endless series of grumbles and complaints such as 'how he would never have agreed to come along if he had known what was involved' and 'Just name me one thing I'm getting out of this?' and - the one that irritates me the most - 'Are we nearly there yet?'

With regard to what he's getting out of it, I remind him that the giant pork pies and chocolate brownies are solely for his benefit and that, left to myself, I would just as soon exist on rough oatcakes and green salads. That's usually enough to shut him up. If there's one thing I'm sure of it's this - there's nothing the bottom half likes so much as a good feed. At times I suspect it's the only thing that keeps him going.

All the same I have to admit he has a point - it can't be very much fun down there; it can be quite wet and the view isn't anything to write home about. Sometimes I find myself admiring the dogged persistence with which the bottom half approaches his task and I like to imagine his efforts are rewarded with some form of brutish gratification . Enduring a few grumbles seems a small price to pay if that's all that's needed to *keep him at it*. Besides, I've found if I pretend I'm not listening he quietens down after a while.

So, on the whole, we get along quite well and though it would be ridiculous to expect the bottom half to come up with much in the conversation department, I am happy to spend some time introducing him to *higher things*. I'm probably fooling myself, but like to think that *something might be going in*.

It was only the other day: I was telling him the story of Robinson Crusoe and I could swear he was listening quite intently.

# Wormwood stumbles upon some-thing

Readers may recall the last Wormwood piece in Over the Wall which was all about my top half and my bottom half and their adventures together on the long walk from Lands End to Cape Wrath. Amongst those people who responded to the item, there were one or two who appeared genuinely alarmed by my dangerous flirtation with the serious matter of a fragmented identity. These people - motivated, I am sure, by a concern for my mental health - explained how the top half and the bottom half are in reality just two aspects of what should be a balanced and harmonious whole and that, by exercising a degree of self-discipline, I might succeed in pulling myself together.

At the risk of causing even greater alarm and concern for my sanity, I have to confess that, as my journey went on, the sense of there being a top half and a bottom half grew stronger with each passing day, to the extent that somewhere around the Scottish Lowlands I began to draw up plans for a contraption that would enable the top half to be almost entirely freed from the more mundane aspects of the journey. This would consist of a sort of desk suspended by straps around the shoulders and similar to the trays used by cinema ice-cream vendors in years gone by. It would need to be big enough to take a laptop computer while leaving room for a phone, a small bookcase and a framed photo of Mrs Wormwood. And though, I have never ridden in one of those boxes mounted on the back of an elephant - howdahs, I think they are called - that is what I imagined it would be like. I even planned to add a little parasol to shield my eyes from the sun.

All in all I got quite excited by the thought of how much useful creative work I might get done (the top half, that is): writing accounts of my journey, replying to emails and so on, while leaving the bottom half to concentrate on the straightforward matter of walking. Of course, I would undoubtedly have to lift my eyes from time to time when the going got rough - either that or risk motion sickness. But then the opportunity to take in my surroundings, to indulge in a few moments of idle reverie would be a welcome distraction. Lulled by the rhythmic swaying I might even allow myself a brief nap.

All of this depending, of course, on the bottom half being relied upon to walk without stumbling, complaining or bickering. A reasonable expectation you might imagine - but then you don't know the bottom half like I do.

It was on the outskirts of Linlithgow that the whole scheme came literally crashing to the ground. We were walking along a good, level path; I was just completing the initial drawings and specifications for the contraption when, suddenly and without warning, I was thrown flat on my face. I was a little shaken, my elbows were grazed and for a moment I thought I might lose a tooth but the real casualty was the very notion that I might be spared any involvement in the mechanics of the journey - an idea which, as was suddenly clear, was a ridiculous fantasy.

It is difficult to accept but it appears that in order to go anywhere, I have to waste valuable time scanning the ground for every tiny stone and tree root. For the simple fact is this - *the bottom half is blind*.

If I'm honest, I think I always knew it.

# Spanish in three months

Mrs Wormwood and I are on holiday in Spain. It is our wedding anniversary today but that's not why we're here - it's just a happy coincidence. We are sitting at a table, by a river, in a little sea port in Asturias. It is lunchtime and we're trying to choose something to eat. Mrs Wormwood fancies the 'Bish of Cheeses'. I for my part, being of a more adventurous nature, am inclined towards the 'Scrambled Egg with an Imitation of Elves made of Fish' - a menu translation that must surely rank amongst the very best examples of the genre and which brings me to the fascinating subject of languages.

A week ago, in preparation for our trip and recognising that there is only so far you can get by speaking very slowly in english, I decided we were going to need some sort of phrase book.

I didn't rate the pocket-sized version on sale in the local newsagents. Apart from costing £4.95 it was full of all sorts of phrases I couldn't see myself needing. Why on earth, for example, would you want to say 'Can we go somewhere quieter' - unless perhaps you were trying to order a drink in a very noisy bar. Neither could I imagine us having any use for the phrase: 'We wish to rent jet-skis'.

No, it was clear - we needed an entirely different sort of phrase book and, as it happened, I found just the thing I was looking for in a secondhand bookshop: Spanish in Three Months, first published in 1969. True, it was a little dog-eared but the thought that it might have nestled in the battered, canvas knapsack of some educated English tramp was immensely appealing.

It was only once we were on holiday and it was too late to do anything about it that I began to realise that this was a very strange phrase book indeed. We were dining out and I was looking for the phrase for 'I can't eat this', which I would have expected to find without too much difficulty. Though there were hundreds, if not thousands, of phrases in the book, none of them seemed quite right. The nearest I could find was 'Throw it out of the window' but I felt this was unnecessarily dramatic. So in the end we pretended we had lost our appetites and went back to our apartment hungry.

Deciding it might be a good idea to be better prepared in future, I sat up late studying Spanish in Three Months and immediately came upon the very phrase I should have used with the restaurant manager earlier in the evening. Gesturing at the food with my knife, I should have asked 'Is this dog yours or your brothers?'. It's a good job I didn't actually say that of course. I mean the kind of unpleasantness likely to have ensued - the sort that culminates in a challenge to a knife-fight in the kitchen alleyway - is something I have always tried my best to avoid.

All the same, Spanish in Three Months turns out to be full of the most wonderful, thought-provoking phrases, the majority of which conjure situations that clearly belong to an earlier, more adventurous time. So, in my imagination, I picture myself on some moonlit Catalonian beach whispering to my must-achioed companion: 'The boxes are nearly all broken and their contents much damaged by water' - a mishap that no doubt might have been avoided had I only taken the time to master the phrase: 'We are thinking of chartering an entire steamer.'

Or there's 'Did you ever go there on horseback?' What mystery; what romance! I long to go on the kind of holiday where I might get to use a phrase like that.

But my favourite by far is the beautifully simple: 'The table is almost in the middle of the room.' Now there's a phrase one might carry around for an entire lifetime and still not find the opportunity to use.

And in case you are wondering, all the phrases mentioned above are to be found in the original 1969 edition of Spanish in Three Months. I can heartily recommend it.

# Pandora's books

As the late Christopher Hitchens once said 'Everybody does have a book in them, but in most cases that is where it should stay.'

We have our great publishing houses to thank for their tireless vigilance in seeing to it that this has remained the case for the last few hundred years. Through unsparing use of the rejection slip, they have succeeded in holding back the deluge of turgid memoirs, dreadful novels and chirpy self-help manuals that otherwise would long since have engulfed us all.

Of course, with the arrival of the Kindle, all that has changed.

Now absolutely anyone with a hard-disk full of idle musings can be instantly transformed into a real writer at the touch of a button. For a tiny modicum of effort you can see your 'book' listed on Amazon, right up there alongside Jamie Oliver and Hilary Mantel and looking every bit as important. There's a nice colour picture of the cover together with your name, the price, the five-star review (kindly written by a friend) and the crucial little button labelled BUY NOW. Except you are the only one who sees the book in this way - for the simple reason that no one else has a cat in hell's chance of finding it, unless they've heard about it already - which of course they haven't.

However many times - in moments of vanity and exaggerated hope – you summon up your book onto your own computer screen, the sad fact remains that you'll be lucky to sell more than a couple of copies, for in reality, your 'book' is buried deep in the bowels of some subterranean Amazon datacentre, alongside hundreds of thousands of similar would-be bestsellers - books with titles such as 'Slug Rearing For Pleasure and Profit' and 'Don't Let Snoring Ruin Your Marriage'.

The individual sales of such books may be tiny but when all of the insignificant trickles are added together they amount to something of a flood of profit for Amazon which of course is why they make it so easy for you to publish your 'book'; not to mention the brilliant marketing ploy of persuading people to buy a specialised Amazon vending machine (called a Kindle) and to carry it around at all times - even to the extent of taking it to bed with them.

Despite all of this, I am confident that my own book - The Wisdom of Wormwood: a collection of the best pieces from Over the Wall (well all of them, to be honest, apart from the one that got me into trouble) and available from Amazon for only £1.99 - will rapidly assume it's natural place near the top of the Amazon sales rankings.

I even hinted to Mrs Wormwood that she might like to start thinking about a new dress for the award ceremony - but she said she'd prefer to wait and see, and that, in any case, the one she bought last autumn for the UK Inventor of the Year - and which she had never worn - would do perfectly well.

She can be terribly cruel sometimes.

# Hobbyism

I have this problem: I get infected with other people's hobbies.

The other day for example, Mrs Wormwood went to visit one of her former work colleagues at her house by the seaside. She took me along to keep the husband busy while she and her friend caught up on the latest news, in that special way that only women ...

Anyway.

No sooner had we exchanged greetings and so on, when the friend said to her husband, in a stage whisper:

'Keith, why don't you show Wormwood your train set.'

'Oh, he won't want to see that!' said Keith.

But I found myself saying: 'Actually I'd love to.' And what's more - I meant it, even as I felt a ripple of mild panic pass through my body.

So Keith and I adjourned to the spare room and it wasn't long before we were hunched over his extensive collection of locomotives.

I was admiring the piston-work on a Robinson D11 when Keith said 'You realise that's the Stephenson valve gear you're looking at there. Lovely, isn't it?'

And suddenly I knew I had to get out – unless, that is, I was willing to risk developing an expensive and time-consuming interest in model railways. I mean, for goodness sake, these things cost a fortune! The Wren model of the Coronation Class 4-6-2 Duchess of Athol, for example, will set you back around £800.

The mere fact that I knew this, was proof enough that it was almost too late. There was nothing else for it but to make our excuses and leave.

Hard on Mrs W though. She and her friend had barely got started. But she's very understanding, Mrs W. She knows I can't help it.

I haven't always got off quite so lightly as I did with the train set. Many's the time I've found myself listening to someone explaining their particular hobby only to find my interest slowly uncoiling like a hungry snake.  And then suddenly it's too late and I'm studying star charts and deciding which astronomical telescope to order.

I'd feel fine about it if I could only settle down with a real hobby and get good at it; but no, by the time I've immersed myself in the details I'm primed and ready for the next infection. And I have had them all:

Wine-making (still in bell-jar after 7 years); stone-carving (lovely set of tools, barely used); Bird-watching (always good to have a pair of binoculars handy); bonsai (they said it was impossible to kill a Chinese Elm); fishing (only cruel if you actually catch fish); card modelling: as well as ships, castles and aeroplanes, you can make a real clock (half-built in cardboard box).

All the same, I will occasionally find myself left with some odd fragments of skill: an ability to play The Moonlight Sonata, for example, or mastery of a single, jaw-dropping magic trick.

Stamp-collecting is an interesting case. Here, rather than acquainting myself with philately in general, I chose to spend the limited time available on developing a detailed knowledge of one tiny corner of the subject, namely the shade variations of the George V First World War definitives. I'll spare you the details but suffice it to say that when visiting London, there's nothing I enjoy more than popping into Stanley Gibbons on The Strand and politely disputing their classification of some of the more difficult penny shades.

The truth is. I am learning to come to terms with my affliction, to accept it as part of who I am. These days I see hobbyism as a natural and healthy lifestyle choice.

Next week I've arranged to visit a man who makes harpsichords. That should keep me busy for a while.

# The invention department

I am sure it will come as no surprise to learn that I'm something of an inventor.

Many are the nights when Mrs Wormwood finds herself forced to dine alone while, from behind the locked cellar door, there comes the faint whirring of machinery, the whistle of compressed air, small explosions and whooshing sounds - all interspersed with exclamations of triumph and so on.

But what exactly has all this activity given rise to?

Well for starters there's the Get-up Grenade™ - an attractively simple gadget designed to appeal to parents of teenage children.

The Get-up Grenade™ is the size and shape of a small ball, fitted with a deafeningly loud alarm, and armed by winding up a powerful internal spring. When the time comes to get ready for school, the busy parent simply opens the teenager's bedroom door and tosses in a Get-up Grenade™ - preferably rolling it under the bed or similar, awkward location. After a short delay the grenade goes off with a loud, high-pitched sound which can only be stopped by a second press of the button.

The product is offered singly or, for parents with several teenage children, as a set of five, in an attractive, vintage leather bandolier.

And, for the high-power executive there's a Desktop Chainsaw – a beautifully engineered and fully functional miniature version of the real thing. Just what's needed for setting the right tone in those difficult one-to-one office situations.

Or how about this one? You've invited friends around for a barbecue and now you're sitting in the balmy evening air enjoying a few drinks, when your guests suddenly find their attention drawn to the sight of bubbles rising to the surface of your modest garden pond.

Next minute they are jumping to their feet in horror and surprise as an enormous scaly back briefly breaks the surface of the water, before gliding silently back into the depths.

There are screams, most probably accompanied by the sound of breaking glass and exclamations along the lines: 'What the ... !'

'Oh yes, I'm so sorry,' you respond languorously, taking another sip of your drink 'I keep meaning to sort that out.'

(The Wormwood Patent Pool Monster™ is operated by a discrete remote control and is available in a size to suit your situation.)

Right now though I'm working on a project aimed at men in their later middle-age who find themselves having to deal with inconvenient and potentially embarrassing failings in the plumbing department.

It's called the hoodie and .....

**Ed:** A word with you, in my office, please Mr Wormwood.

# Ripe thoughts

Elderly readers of Over the Wall will no doubt recall the cinema actor Victor Mature and his starring role in Cecil B. DeMille's masterpiece: Samson and Delilah, in which Mr Mature plays opposite that smouldering sex-bomb, Hedy Lamarr.

I don't believe I ever saw a man who could pull-off (as it were) a ripped, leather loincloth quite as well as Victor Mature. All the same, I never could understand how Mature was considered a good name for a really sexy man. It just doesn't convey the right qualities.

Hedy Lamarr, on the other hand, is an extremely sexy name, especially when pronounced with a Manchester accent and with the last syllable prolonged, like a drawn-out, wistful sigh.

No, if you're going to dream up a good name for a big, passionate guy with massive pecs, Victor Mature is not a good choice. You might just as well call him Ted Sensible and be done with it.

Maturity is a quality intended to suggest quiet strength, sophistication and experience. The mature individual is thought to be at the very high point of life's journey. Or at least that's the idea. More likely it's just a gentle way of saying 'old' - like an old, smelly cheese.

Such were the thoughts that ran through my head as I pondered what on earth there is to say about maturity beyond the fact that it is a highly dangerous condition that can sneak up on a person without warning. To check whether you are at risk, simply answer the following five questions:

1.  Towards the end of a music concert do you find yourself anticipating the inevitable encore and hoping that they'll not be too long getting on with it as you're already secretly looking forward to a cup of horlicks, a warm bed and a good night's sleep?

2.  Is this you? On arriving at someone else's house after a long car journey, not only do you turn down the offer of wine, with the words 'No thanks, but I'd love a cup of tea' but you simultaneously shame all of your companions - who are desperate for a drink – into following your example.

3.  Do you suspect that - for some mysterious and incomprehensible reason - they have decided to stage the Grand National twice a year (ditto The Boat Race, Last Night of the Proms, Christmas etc)?

4.  If you were to discover that your friends and colleagues thought of you as 'mature' would this make you happy?

5.  Do you have a party piece prepared that you can deliver at short notice if called upon to do so?

Answer yes to three or more of the above and you should seek immediate help.

# Smell-checkers

Of all the truly marvelous technological innovations that nowadays enrich our lives, the spell-checker is surely one of the most beneficial. After all, what could be more heart-breaking than to see a perfectly sound piece of writing utterly devalued, purely on account of poor spelling.

As is now widely accepted, difficulties with spelling should not be taken to indicate impaired intelligence or creativity. It is not widely known, but both Agatha Christie and Gustave Flaubert couldn't spell for toffee. Fortunately they had amanuenses to help them out. Nowadays, thanks to the smell-checker, we can all enjoy a similar degree of literary confident.

All the same, as is soften the case with radical innovations, there are people who, out of ignorant, fear or predicate, would have us turn our backs on this wonderful boom. One school of thought is happy to accept smell-checking but draws the lime at auto-collection, arguing that the latter risks robbing us, not only of our swords, but of the very ideas that under spin them. It is one thing to be averted to the fact that you have made a smelling mistake; it is quite another to have some completely random word hoisted upon you. People can become so valiant on spell checkers - so these alarmists claim - that they no longer have the fastest clue as to whether the worms appearing on the scream are the ones they meant to write - all they know is that they are spelled corrects.

Another common objection is that we are increase and singly wallowing electron technocracy to take control of what we communicate to otters - with truly tightening embrocations. Identity heft is usually mistaken as the risk that our personal details might be stolen by hacketts, coincidence tricksters and other criminals. On the contrary - so the unguent goes - it will be our own increasingly clever computers and mobile homes that will empty our bank amounts and cause us to be falsely abused of all sorts of unspeakable chimes.

At the extreme end, there are those who put about the paranoid fear that, despise our best tuffets, the words we writhe will soon no longer make any sense a tall and that - like streetwalkers - we risk slithering inexorably back into the dark cages.

Personal I consider all such backward-smoking worries unruly pepsi-mystic and uttermost without foundations.

# Domestic science

Ask a group of people to tell you what they understand by the term 'domestic science' and most will say how it's the stuff that girls do at school while the boys are making wooden tea trays. Things like ironing table-cloths and writing thankyou letters.

I am reluctant to admit it, but I fear that Mrs Worm-wood might be somewhat of this persuasion.

For me, on the other hand, domestic science means real, big-boy science which just happens to be carried out in the home.

Take the Van de Graaf generator, for example.

To be honest, when I first picked it up on eBay I didn't have a clue what I was going to do with it – at least not till that party just before Christmas, the one that made everyone's hair stand on end.

Starting with a group of old friends and a 5 megavolt Van de Graaf generator, you just add a sprinkle of alcohol and bingo - you have an electrifying party. It wasn't long before they became something of a regular occurrence round at our place

I recall one such evening. The air was crackling, the dial was 'turned up to eleven' and the sparks were starting to fly when, like a bolt out of the blue, it came to me: the most stupendously brilliant idea I have ever had and one that, besides promising scientific acclaim, honours and accolades, would likely be rewarded with fabulous wealth.

Shut your eyes and imagine for a moment. You are slumped on the sofa at home after an exhausting day at the office. Unhooking your attention momentarily from the TV screen, you gaze wistfully at a herd of tiny elephants, as they shuffle their way across the carpet.

This was my vision; this is what I decided I would give to the world -- perfect, miniature elephants.

Later, Mrs Wormwood told me that, though I was unconscious for no more than two or three minutes, she was starting to get worried and that if I *must* persist in my scientific explorations then perhaps it could be a little more of the David Attenborough and a bit less of the Victor Frankenstein.

I promised her I would try. To be honest I was starting to get bored with the Van de Graaf generator parties anyway.

And so, for these past twelve weeks I have barely left my workshop. I spent the first four Googling everything I could find on gene-splicing, cell cultures and so on and the next four ordering equipment: centrifuges, mass spectrometers and lots of plastic tubing. Since then I have been working so hard I can't have slept for more than 15 minutes at a time. Just a few more nights and I should be ready to launch the fruits of my endeavours.

I have already secretly bought Mrs Wormwood something to wear at the press conference. I hope she likes it. It is a long black T-shirt on which the following words are written in bold, white letters

**PLEASE
HELP ME!
I AM BEING
HELD HOSTAGE
BY A
CRAZY PERSON**

which will be really funny, as everyone knows how
devoted to me she is.

# Time's unstoppable flow

I can't be the only one to have noticed that time has begun to speed up at an alarming rate. As if growing older weren't enough of a challenge without suddenly discovering that another whole year has flashed by in what – in one's childhood – would have been the space of a single summer's day.

It's a bit like those people who go over the edge of the Niagara Falls in a barrel – you know: the accelerating rush, the deafening roar, the helplessness as they are drawn toward the foaming brink.

**Readers:** 'Goodness – did they survive?'

Personally, I prefer to think of myself as one who, rather than trusting to the mercy of time's cruel current, chooses to swim against it, like a magnificent salmon leaping through the tumbling rapids.

**Readers:** 'I guess they didn't make it, eh?'

Who?

**Readers:** 'The guys in the barrel.'

Forget the guys in the barrel; I'm sharing some of my best insights here.

For example, it has been shown that, when it comes to resisting time's inexorable course, one of the best strategies is to set about acquiring a new skill. It might be learning to speak a foreign language, playing a musical instrument or mastering a juggling trick.

There is one crucial point to remember however and it is this: on no account must you be tempted to allow curiosity to develop into an actual proficiency. Quite apart from the fact that you will undoubtedly discover the whole business to be far more complicated than you first thought, the fact is you simply *don't have the time* to sit back and practice your new found skill.

Or, as all good hedge-fund managers will tell you:

*'Never trade today's reality for tomorrows potential'*

**Readers:** 'It's fine for you to talk about forgetting but once you've planted an image like that it takes some shaking off.'

I take it you're still on about the barrel here?

**Readers:** 'The slow, strangely silent fall followed by the inevitable, sickening impact'

Oh, for goodness sake. Who is meant to be writing this piece?

OK, have it your own way: they all went over the edge and I'm not sure any of them survived.

**Readers:** 'It is just as we feared.'

I am beginning to regret ever bringing up the subject.

# Back to the future

I am the first to admit that Mrs Wormwood is a great driver. She's so good in fact that, whenever we're in the car together, I'm perfectly happy to sit back and give myself over to daydreaming. This arrangement suits Mrs Wormwood too - so we're both happy.

Picture the scene -- we might have been to a wedding in Yorkshire, for example, and now we're driving back over the Pennines or, to be accurate, Mrs Wormwood is driving and I am slipping into one of my favourite fantasies: the one where I imagine Sir Isaac Newton, dead for almost 300 years, has been miraculously brought back to life, restored to something like the state of awareness he enjoyed when he last graced this earth. And as he has missed out on the industrial revolution, the internal combustion engine and the development of the Playstation 3, I have been selected from amongst the world's citizens, to bring him up to speed.

So here we are, gliding along the M62, as the delicate violet and green tones of the western sky slowly give way to the twinkling phosphorescent ocean that marks out Manchester and the Lancashire mill towns. Sir Isaac is in the back, crouched down and gripping the edges of my seat like someone caught up in an earthquake. It takes me all of 20 minutes to reassure him that the strange crystal and resinous capsule, in which he finds himself, is not careening out of control but -- on the contrary -- responds faithfully to the deft manipulation of an ingenious system of foot pedals.

Later, after he has found the courage to peep out from behind the seat, I set about patiently explaining the science of electricity – covering the basic principles of power generation and distribution in some detail, before going on to hint at the fascinating fields of analogue and digital electronics.

I was expecting him to respond with all sorts of interesting questions. Instead, he simply gazes open-mouthed at the torrents of living light -- ruby red and white -- as they stream over sinuous ribbons of tarmac. Perhaps I'll wait for a while before showing him my mobile phone.

The truth is, I am starting to get a bit bored by Sir Isaac. Reckon I'll swap him for Johann Sebastian Bach. That should keep me going till we get to the M5.

With Bach – along with the technology stuff – the fun part is deciding how to get from the The Art of Fugue to hip-hop without him trying to jump out of the car.

*'That's right Johann Sebastian; you put these little pearls into your ears and then you touch your finger to this glowing hieroglyph and .... wooahh, easy now !'*

# Christmas with the Ecclestones

Despite the fact that, generally speaking, we are 'not at home to Mr Murdoch', there appears to be little I can do to prevent Santa from including a copy of Hello Magazine in Mrs Wormwood's Christmas stocking.

Despite feigning disapproval, I have to admit there's something strangely comforting about snuggling down after a good Christmas dinner to leaf through the pages of Hello and its parade of wastrels, poseurs, musk-cats and prick-me-dainties all set off against a backdrop of grotesque interior decoration.

And besides - it is good to be reminded that the people in Hello magazine have real human feelings and emotions just like the rest of us. So, for example, it's lovely to know that Tamara Ecclestone and her partner, having decided to trade the British cold for the warmer temperatures in Dubai, chose to delay their Christmas Day flight till the late afternoon, simply in order to have the whole Christmas morning 'chilling in their specially bought Christmas jumpers'.

It's not like life at the top is all a bed of roses either. Articles in Hello magazine regularly include obscure references as to how so-and-so is 'battling with demons' - which doesn't sound very nice.

Mrs Wormwood tells me that this is not to be taken literally – as some sort of titanic struggle with the forces of Beelzebub – but is a figure of speech discretely hinting at a form of addiction or compulsive behaviour such as an over-fondness for Maltesers, excessive shopping or killing wild animals - all of which, nevertheless, must be very trying.

Whatever else we might think of it, Hello magazine serves a valuable and admirable purpose in helping raise our eyes above the tawdry and inconsequential trivialities of our own boring lives and encouraging us to aspire to better things. It is comforting to think that with just a little bit more effort and entrepreneurialism, we too might enjoy a palatial home set in 900 acres of parkland along with a trophy 'love of our life' and an adorable baby. The people who already have these things come all too often from humble beginnings and if they can heave and claw themselves out of the common slime then surely we can too.

This year I found the touching story of Princess Gloria von Thurn and Taxis especially moving. After the sudden and unexpected death of her ancient husband, Gloria found herself suddenly threatened with the loss of her 500-room home. Employing what she describes as her 'simple, motherly, household accounting brain' and cutting down on the parties, shopping trips, African safaris etc., she set about 'living within her means' with exemplary and uncomplaining stoicism. Despite these admirable efforts, she was eventually forced to endure the indignity of auctioning off her jewels at Sotheby's along with 75,000 bottles of vintage wine, just in in order to make ends meet. She now lives a life of austerity and selfless piety - starting each day with a personal Mass in her private chapel.

I confess, I found the whole piece immensely touching and a welcome reminder that, whatever our own difficulties, there are those who soldier on with a quiet, uncomplaining dignity - an example and inspire-ation to us all.

# Cornish drama

To: Rebecca Eaton: Executive Producer, Poldark

Dear Ms Eaton,

Please allow me to congratulate you on an absolutely splendid drama – quite simply the best thing that Mrs Wormwood and I have seen on TV since Downton Abbey. It is the highlight of our Sunday evening's entertainment.

Every aspect of the production – from the Cornish locations, the carefully researched and meticulously tailored costumes, to the sumptuous interiors of Trenwith (set in our own cherished Chavenage House) – all are combined to breath-taking effect.

But it is in the casting that one detects an assurance that is little short of genius.

I confess I first thought Aidan Turner a little too outrageously good-looking to be convincing as Ross Poldark but Mrs Wormwood assures me he's just perfect.

And, in casting Heida Reed as Elizabeth Chenoweth, how mischievously you toyed with our emotions. With her finely-sculpted features, she appeared too well-bred to serve as the principal love interest and so it proved – for that part is wonderfully and touchingly claimed by Demelza, played by Eleanor Tomlinson, whose simple English beauty perfectly chimes with modern sensibilities.

One could go on: Jack Farthing as George Warleggan - living proof that as long as there are parts for unscrupulous bastards with drooping eyelids and cruel lips he is unlikely to find himself out of work; or Ruby Bentall as the kind-hearted spinster, Verity. Simply brilliant.

But of course, it is the compelling storyline that really marks Poldark out as an absolutely top-rate drama. A touching romance set in a community in which ruthless entrepreneurs and pitiless financiers pursue their selfish interests against a backdrop of poverty and degradation – what could be more relevant to our own times?

And so it was especially gratifying in the latest episode to find - following the discovery of copper in the Poldark mine - that things are about to get a whole lot better for Ross and Demelza.

Which brings me to the main point of this letter.

For in the scene where Ross Poldark talks to Demelza on returning from the shareholders' meeting, Mrs Wormwood and I couldn't help noticing an attractive set of six pewter plates arranged on the dresser he's leaning against - I trust you will not think it too forward of me - but as you're no doubt planning to exchange their humble farmhouse for a more elegant dwelling and furnish it with fine brocades, porcelain tea services and the like, we were wondering whether you had any further use for them - the pewter plates, that is. As we expect to be visiting Cornwall in the next few weeks, it would be a simple matter to pick them up in person.

I do hope that future episodes will not produce any unforeseen setbacks as we have also set our hearts on the antique carved oak settle that features in the scene in which Demelza sits sewing with Verity and that would be just perfect for our new kitchen extension. We can collect it at the same time.

Yours (in eager anticipation of a favourable reply),

William Wormwood

# Glastonbury report

So I have been to Glastonbury to find out what all the fuss is about and, though my stay was shorter than planned, I can state with some confidence that it is a complete shambles.

The first thing that struck me was that there were an awful lot of people there and, to make matters worse, they seemed constantly to be on the move. Though the organisers have provided a number of rough tracks for people to walk along there is absolutely no attention given to traffic management. Even the most rudimentary protocols, such as asking people to keep to the left, are entirely lacking. The situation is not helped by a common tendency for groups of people to stand idly chatting, right in the middle of the flow of festival-goers, apparently insensible to the fact they are causing an obstruction. I lost count of the times I tried politely asking people to step to one side, only to be met with responses ranging from dumb incredulity to outright verbal abuse.

If moving around is something of a nightmare, it is at the various outdoor musical concerts that things get utterly ridiculous. One of the more regrettable tendencies – seen especially near the front of the crowd – is for young women to sit astride the shoulders of their boyfriends and to wave their arms about, utterly obscuring the view of the stage for those unfortunate enough to be standing behind them. Even the performers appear to disapprove of this selfish behaviour. One particular singer, descending to a lower platform, walked from one end to the other, pointing at the worst offenders and shouting:

*'Get down, get down. Everybody get down'*

all of which only provoked them to even wilder fits of arm-waving. He might as well have been talking to a brick wall.

Concluding – if somewhat reluctantly -- that attempting to bring some semblance of order to the Pyramid Stage was beyond my limited resources, I decided to turn my attention to the various small booths and sideshows that are dotted around the site in large numbers. Of these, by far the most bizarre was a strange cluster of marquees and fenced off enclosures run by a man dressed as a rabbit. This was immensely popular, as was apparent from the long queue of people waiting to gain admission -- which they were required to do through a tunnel so small as to force them to crawl on hands and knees.

Inside, a lot of strange people in outlandish costumes were lounging around chatting, seemingly oblivious to the fact that the music they were listening to was clearly stuck in a loop. I attempted to point this out to the rabbit man but he seemed incapable of stopping still for more than two seconds. So in the end – out of sheer desperation -- I decided to resort to the tried and tested remedy of giving the amplification equipment a hefty kick, which instantly fixed the problem, if at the minor expense of causing the music to stop completely.

To say that my initiative was not appreciated by the organisers would be an understatement and I quickly found myself outside again, though thankfully not via the tunnel this time but through a far more practical back door.

No – as is clear to me now – if Glastonbury is to have a future there will need to be some fundamental changes, such as siting it on a disused airfield where the tents can be pitched in orderly rows separated by straight, well-surfaced tracks -- all of which I patiently explained to the people up at the police compound whilst waiting for them to fix me up with a lift home.

Mrs Wormwood -- who had been enjoying a quiet weekend -- seemed unsurprised by my early return, saying only:

'*Oh please, not again.*'

# Unspeakable emotions

As you may be aware, your humble servant is something of a polymath - being generally at home amongst the higher reaches of mathematics, philosophy and the natural sciences. But there again, considering my natural modesty, reluctance to beat my own drum etc., it's possible the fact has escaped you.

Be that as it may: earlier this week my attention was drawn to a fascinating piece in New Scientist that explained how there are certain emotions for which there is no word in English but for which there is a perfectly good word in some other language. So, for example, there's **Iktsuarpok** – an Inuit word that describes the fidgety feeling when visitors are due to arrive (and which incidentally we might usefully adopt to describe the compulsion constantly to check our phones for that hoped-for text message). Then there's **Amae**, which for Japanese people refers to the pleasure and trust in surrendering to hugs and cuddles.

The article goes on to suggest that we might be completely incapable of feeling emotions that we don't have a word for. However, I don't believe this for a moment. Take **Schadenfreude** for example, which in German refers to the sense of delight in another's misfortune. Just because we're too nice in this country to admit such a shameful emotion exists, it doesn't mean we haven't all secretly enjoyed its pleasures.

One of my own personal favourites is **Sehnsucht** – the sense of yearning or wistful longing which in my case usually kicks in around mid-September. The Portuguese word **Saudade** apparently has much the same meaning, as does the Romanian word: **Dor** – which sums up the feeling perfectly, in just three letters.

Anyway, all of this has got me thinking and I reckon there's a whole stack of emotions for which there are no words in any language (at least not until now, that is) but which are no less real for all that. Here are a few that spring to mind: some shameful, others entirely innocent.

Inconsomnia: The sadness felt on waking from a dream in which you have [won the lottery], [rekindled a lost love], [discovered you can fly].

Procrastitude: The despondency arising from the realisation that, having put off starting a task, you no longer have a hope of completing it.

Unboxstacy: The sense of rapture that follows on from the purchase of a brand new consumer product.

Grudgery: Resentment arising from being forced to feign enthusiasm – as experienced, for example, when invited to watch a 2-hour video of your nephew's school sportsday.

Stuffocation: The panicky feeling brought on by the realisation that you are no longer capable of throwing *anything* away.

Duwuwu: The cosiness and security experienced when sheltering from the wind.

**Waitrage:** Suppressed antagonism felt towards fellow customers at a well-known, high-class supermarket -- on account of their cars, contents of their trolleys, tendency to amble down the aisles clutching their free cups of coffee.

And finally -- one submitted by Mrs Wormwood --

**Solus:** The wave of euphoria experienced on returning home to find that one has the house to oneself.

# Psychotyping

One of my favourite comic writers - 'the soles of whose shoes I am unworthy to lick' (to quote Eric Idle) - was Paul Jennings. Some of his best pieces were published as a collection called The Jenguin Pennings. If you have ever read any of these you might have noticed a certain similarity to the infinitely more humble offerings of your very own Wormwood. There's no secret about it; Paul Jennings was a great insulation. (I meant to say 'inspiration' of course, but the spell-checker decided it knew better).

All of which reminds me of one of my favourite Jennings pieces. As is customary he starts with something quite innocuous before letting his comic imagination get to work. In this case he was learning to touch type and, in particular, typing the standard test phrase: 'the quick brown fox jumps over the lazy dog'. Forbidden to look at the keys, he inevitably made mistakes and then went on to analyse them for hidden, subconscious significance.

Of course, the spell-checker gives the whole enterprise a turbot boat - or should I say a turbo boost - and so I decided to give it a try.

Using Hamlet's famous soliloquy as the test piece, I typed it out as fast as I could with the spell-checker turned up to 11.

Here's what emerged:

*To be or not ego end; that is the quiet son.*

And you see how, right from the word go, we're into

some pretty deep stuff. That 'ego end' for example. What more profound way to talk about death?

> *Whether it is an oblige in the mind to suffer the Swiss and arrows of outrageous rotund …*

This is undoubtedly more difficult. 'An oblige in the mind' has something primitive about it - there are hints here of a subconscious compulsion, but quite what the Swiss have to do with it is unclear.

> *Or to take absinthe and sea-dog trailers and, by opening, end them.*

Stranger and stranger. Despite the fact that a sea-dog trailer is exactly the sort of thing you might expect to come across after a dose of absinthe, it is utterly incomprehensible why you should want to open them and how that is going to help anything.

This was clearly going to demand some serious analysis; I decided to try something simpler:

> *Humpy dimply dat one a wall.*
> *Humphrys de dumpty had agreed to a fall*
> *All the kinda horse and all the makings men*
> *Couldn't pry Humply together again.*

which I am sure you will agree can confidently hold its own against the original.

As to what it means exactly - I will leave you to decide.

# CUUEG

A letter landed on the mat this morning inviting me to the 50th anniversary reunion of the Cambridge University Underwater Exploration Group and I found my thoughts drifting back across the years to the days when I was briefly numbered amongst its members.

Not for us the modern buoyancy compensator, balanced-piston regulator, or semi-closed rebreather. No - a pair of waxed canvas trousers, lead boots and an inflated sheeps bladder was all we needed to explore the watery domain.

But joking aside, I vividly recall my first (and nearly last) open-water dive with the CUUEG.

Dropping off the edge of an inflatable dinghy, off Mousehole in Cornwall, I sank like a stone to a depth of 30 metres. After crawling around in the kelp for a while, we came up again - which I remember enjoying on account of the feeling of floating in a bright void.

Later in the week one of our instructors had the opportunity to spend a couple of days inside a naval recompression chamber.

I later discovered that his status as an instructor amounted to the fact that he had survived the previous year's trip AND that he had decided to repeat the experience.

I didn't dive again for 25 years.

Though I don't plan to attend the 50th anniversary celebrations, I extend my heartfelt greetings to fellow survivors. I am sure it is all very different nowadays.

# Luxury trends

I was shocked yesterday to read of the decline in sales of luxury handbags. We might be going through a bit of a sticky patch at the moment, but when all is said and done, we're talking about handbags for goodness sake - not luxury yachts.

You can't tell me that the sort of person who was prepared to pay £11,000 for a Burberry handbag last year is any poorer today - or at least not in any way that makes sense to the rest of us.

No – there is something else going on here.

I suspect the reason for the decline - and it's not just handbags; apparently the blight extends to watches, haute couture, lamborghinis and so on - is that it's no longer quite cool to be seen flaunting this kind of stuff. On a more day-to-day level, who hasn't glanced at the suddenly ridiculous 4x4 in the supermarket car park all smoked-glass and bull-bar, and quietly thought:

*'Loser !'*

Incidentally, while researching this piece, I came across an organisation called The Luxury Institute – motto:

*The Knowledge of Luxury, the Luxury of Knowledge.*

On their web page they declare that:

> *'As the luxury industry enters 2009, some luxury executives look like deer caught in the headlights.'*

Lovely touch that - how, even in metaphor, the luxury institute feels compelled to enlist the help of a superior animal. Rabbits in the headlights might be good enough for the rest of us but for the luxury executive only the finest deer will suffice.

I can't resist just one further quote from this priceless web site:

> '... we now also expect many discredited Wall Street executives to turn a new leaf in an effort to save family legacies and reputations and get into **the high-end philanthropy game** (my emphasis). It's not much fun for kids to have the wealthiest parents in private school when everyone knows they made their money in a Ponzi scheme that brought the world economy to its knees.'

Quite. I couldn't agree more; it must be absolutely frightful for them. So brace yourselves for photo shoots of celebrities, dressed in the latest recycled clothing, doing a stint on the soup kitchen:

> 'In times like these, we must all share the pain, blah blah.'

# Respect the geek

Though I don't exactly consider myself a geek, I have to confess to certain tendencies in that direction.

I don't believe I could have spent the last 25 years of my life writing computer programs AND considered it fun for more than 50% of the time AND chosen to use this sort of language to register these facts, were it not for the likelihood that, when it comes to my place on the autistic spectrum, I turn out to be somewhere near the blue end.

All the same, when it comes to geeks, I'm nothing special. It's true - I enjoy mathematical puzzles, I have a small stamp collection and read tool catalogues but I also like paintings and other forms of art and have been known, at times, to hold strong political views.

Being only a minor geek; being merely ... geekish, I think of myself as a kind of channel between the two worlds: the geek world - the world of knowledge, of delight in detail, discipline (in the monkish sense) and uncomplicated friendships and the other one, the world that most people seem to want to belong to - the world of flamboyance, fluffiness, studied-incompetence and clumsily-constructed explanations.

Of course, it is common knowledge that geeks score very highly when it comes to complicated technical matters. Such things could be said to constitute their principle source of pleasure - which is fortunate for the rest of us, as it should be clear by now that it's the geeks who are keeping the whole show on the road. You only have to think for a short while about what keeps the electricity on, what keeps your mobile phone working or about having television AT ALL, to realise that neither you, nor anyone else you know has the faintest inkling about how it all fits together.

You might expect the geek to demand a very high level of reward for carrying out these critically important functions, but you'd be mistaken. A liberal dress-code, freedom from petty distractions and a plentiful supply of pizzas are generally sufficient to keep things ticking along.

And while honours and public acclaim might seem entirely reasonable expectations - to the geek sensibility, simple acknowledgment of the true state of things would be recognition enough. Sadly, even the most modest level of respect is rarely forthcoming.

It is as if awareness of the fact that our daily existence rests in the hands of train-spotters and dungeon-quest experts is too much to take on board - with the consequence that geeks are all to often the object of derision; their harmless enthusiasms ridiculed, their awkwardness in social situations mercilessly mocked.

This would all be terribly sad were it not for the fact that geeks have a characteristically geekish way of getting their own back. It draws on a shared, esoteric knowledge of a geek sacred text - Douglas Adams: A Hitchhiker's Guide to the Galaxy.

Amongst other tales, the book recounts how the inhabitants of the planet Golgafrincham, on resolving to rid themselves of a third of their population they consider completely useless, concoct a story that the planet is shortly to be destroyed in a great catastrophe. They persuade all the hairdressers, insurance salesmen, personnel officers, management consultants, telephone sanitisers and hedge-fund managers to board the B-Ark - one of three giant spaceships - and promise them that everyone else will follow shortly in the other two.

And so it was that in the various offices and research centres, where I spent a good slice of my life engaged in geek work, the unwelcome interference of opinionated, self-important people would be met by a knowing exchange of glances and by the quiet intonation of the simple mantra: 'B-Ark'

# Bottomless pits

There were a lot of abandoned mineshafts around where I grew up in the north of England - chilling vertical holes, lined with millstone grit and quite often completely unprotected by the usual fences and skull and crossbones signs.

Being of a somewhat philosophical frame of mind, I found it difficult to resist peering cautiously down into the inky depths while terrifying myself with the thought of how very easy it would be to pitch myself in. Far better to lob down a sizeable rock and count the seconds before it hit the bottom with echoes either of deep water or the sharp crack of shattered stone. The depth of the shaft was then readily calculated by means of the familiar formula: depth (in feet) equals 16 times the delay (in seconds) squared.

Except occasionally there was no sound from the bottom but only a succession of ever feinter scrapes as the plunging rock grazed the shaft walls. The inescapable conclusion was that these were bottomless pits and it was a good idea to move on and, above all, to resist any further thoughts of having a second look down.

When I come to think of it, bottomless pits seemed to feature quite strongly in my boyish imagination.

Of course, the real explanation was that the stone had simply thudded softly and inaudibly into a pile of dead sheep and old mattresses.

Anyone who has tried writing a blog will immediately know what I'm talking about ...

# Spooky digital clocks

These days it seems that every time I look at a digital clock it's either 4:44, 22:22 or some other time where the digits are all identical.

I don't mean every single time of course - that would be seriously creepy. No, I mean like once a day. Certainly more often than you'd expect.

Let's do the sums: In the case of a 12-hour clock the number of distinct time displays is 12 times 60 - or 720. Of these, the ones with identical digits are 1:11, 2:22, 3:33, 4:44, 5:55 and 11:11. So in a 12 hour period you expect to see one of these 6 single-digit patterns 6 times for every 720 looks at the clock (or 1 in 120).

For a 24-hour clock, we can add 0:00 and 22:22 but the other numbers only come up once, so we have 8 cases out of 1440 (or 1 in 180).

In either case it means that to see one or more of these patterns every day suggests that I look at the clock more than 120 times in a 24 hour period. Not counting the time I am asleep that works out about once every 8 minutes. Surely I can't be doing that!

Perhaps you'll understand now why I find it all a bit spooky. In fact it has given me a really good idea for a low-budget horror movie:

**Scene 1:**   Man rolls over in bed. Sleepily notes the time on bedside clock. It says 2:22

**Scene 2:** Alarm clock rings. 5:55 on the display. Daylight filters through the curtains. Radio announces tragic motorway accident.

**Scene 3:** Man driving through city, stuck in slow-moving traffic.
Clock on car radio shows 3:33.
Suddenly a panic-stricken woman claws frantically at the car door, face momentarily pressed to the glass.

**Scene 4:** Man driving along motorway, shaken by the recent encounter and lost in thought.
Clock says 4:44.
He doesn't appear to notice.

**Scene 5:** It begins to rain.
Man peers through windscreen. Strange lights ahead.
Clock says **6:66** !!
Cue Psycho-type music.
Man's mouth formed into silent scream. Screeching of car brakes, rending of tortured metal.

Cut to credits against background of flashing blue lights reflected in wet tarmac.

If you've read this far, it's probably too late; you're going to start waking up and noticing it's 11:11.

Aaagghhh !

Sorry.

# Radio 4 Today rage

The news that 29 senior managers in the UK Border Agency are to be paid bonuses averaging £10,000 each as a reward for, to quote the immigration minister Phil Woolas: *'delivering what the government is asking them to do'*, leads me to speculate on their baseline job description:

- You will be expected to carry out your duties with no worse than mild to moderate incompetence.

- With respect to negligence or serious professional misconduct, there must be no more than one such episode in any 12 month period.

- Patronising behaviour, verbal abuse, sexual harassment and non-physical bullying will be tolerated, provided these are kept within reasonable limits and can be shown to be compatible with corporate goals.

- And finally, at at time when many ordinary working families are facing unprecedented challenges to their security and standard of living, you will be expected to lead and motivate a team of 25,000 front-line staff by fostering an environment of mutual respect and shared values.

**Reader:** I thought you said you were going to cut down on this kind of thing?

**Omnivorist:** I know. It's just ... I get this sort of red mist.

**Reader:** For goodness sake! Try and get a grip on yourself.

# Ear worms

As if it isn't enough to suffer the distressing effects of horological monodigitism[1], I find myself plagued by a new problem - a mild form of obsessive compulsive disorder with musical manifestations (OCDM2).

I can think of no better explanation than to describe a typical episode.

I'll be enjoying the recollection of one of my favourite pieces of music - let's say Liszt's Fifth Hungarian Rhapsody - when I suddenly become aware that I have been whistling the same 4 or 5 bars under my breath for most of the morning. By the next day it has taken a firm hold and I find myself replaying the same loop in my imagination, more or less unconsciously.

It's easy to put the tune aside once I become aware that I am playing it, but it has a sneaky tendency to start up again as soon as my back is turned. It's not unusual for a single tune to get lodged for 4 or 5 days, with occasional episodes lasting anything up to a month.

'Aha', I hear you clamouring to suggest: 'Why don't you just think of a different piece of music ?'.

If only it were that simple.

Certainly using one tune to drive out another is a sensible strategy. But consider this. There are only certain tunes capable of displacing one that has outstayed its welcome. The tunes you'd like to recall -

---

[1] Spooky digital clocks

the one's you're particularly fond of - they always turn out to be useless.

Just before Christmas, for example, I had a particularly persistent fixation with Happiness (by Goldfrapp). Now, on the whole, I consider this to be an intelligent and appealing piece of music but after two weeks of uninterrupted mental playback I was beginning to find it tiresome.

I tried a couple of alternatives. The Byrds: Eight Miles High - that classic from the very zenith of Californian hippy culture - never really got much of a hold. Much more promising was Friday Night and Saturday Morning (the Nouvelle Vague version featuring Daniella D'Ambrosio). I've worked with it in the past and know from experience that, while very effective as a musical purgative, it can be a devil to get rid of once it's got its feet under the table. But - mercifully perhaps - it didn't take on this occasion.

So I was stuck with the Goldfrapp for a few days more before I did what I knew I'd be forced to do all along.

You see there's a fiendishly subtle twist to this particular neurosis that makes one suspect it to be the work of some malevolent intelligence. It is this. While there is no particular difficulty in identifying a tune to do the business - it will invariably be one that is both more banal and persistent than the tune it displaces.

So, out of desperation, I forced out the Goldfrapp with Jesus Wants me for Sunbeam which I endured for an afternoon before resorting to Puff the Magic Dragon.

Beyond this point the choice suddenly becomes quite limited as there are only a handful of tunes that are sufficiently fatuous to deal with Puff the Magic Dragon. Of course, there's always The Chicken Song - but that could be regarded as overkill. No, there's really only one candidate as far as I'm concerned and that's Lily the Pink (by The Scaffold).

Some might regard the fact that this song topped the UK singles chart for 4 whole weeks in 1968 as no more than a minor cultural footnote. For my part, I consider it as clear evidence of a significant public health risk.

# A man after my own heart

I'm thinking of David Cheval - who proposes on the BBC PM programme that cigarette manufacturers should be required (by law) to wrap filters in fluorescent pink paper (in contrast to the faux cork-effect paper they currently favour) and all in the interests of shaming  smokers into disposing of their dog-ends more responsibly.

On hearing his letter read out on the PM program, he dashes into his wife:

> *'Darling, they read my letter! All those years of campaigning, the indifference, the derision. You know, at times, I've even begun to doubt  myself (laughs, uncontrollably). But now, now! Oh I must make plans - I must think, think, think !'*

> *(Digs fingertips into temples).*

> *'First thing tomorrow, phone the Director General or - no, no - Eddie Mair, should let him share the credit - mustn't get carried away.'*

> *'But it's so exciting; we're going to do this! First thing tomorrow we're going to email every MP ....'*

Mrs Cheval (staring blankly into her drink)

> *'And here was I thinking how he was getting better ....'*

Meanwhile, in the Radio 4 studio:

> *'Night Lucy.'*

> *'Night Eddie.'*

'Great one tonight, by the way, Lucy.'

'Oh … what?'

'The nutcase with the fluorescent cigarette butts. Just perfect for a friday night. Nothing like a laugh to soothe away the cares of the week. Have a good weekend.'

# Everyday design No 1: The sardine tin.

I was leafing through the January 1924 edition of Popular Mechanics the other day when I came across the following fascinating piece:

### Opening Sardine Tins

Anyone who has opened a sardine tin knows that while it is very easy to roll back the cover by means of the key until  it is in the position shown in the illus- tration, it requires a very powerful pres- sure on the key to force the rolled cover past the corner of the tin. If, however, when this point is reached, the point of an ice pick, or similar tool, is inserted through the handle of the key in the manner indicated, a leverage is provided that makes it very easy to strip off the remainder of the cover. This kink will be appreciated by the feminine members of the family, whose fingers are not strong enough to apply the necessary force to the key.

Ah ... many are the days I fished just such a tin out of my duffel bag while sitting at the end of a chilly railway platform in autumn waiting for the Euston to Man- chester Piccadilly to come through (even though it was more often than not pulled by nothing more exciting than a humble 4-6-0 Stanier.)

And of course I am only too familiar with the dilemma depicted in the above article - though I have to admit, I rarely had an ice-pick to hand and, most times, had to content myself with leaving the tin half-open and teasing out the sardines with a lolly stick.

But despite the fact that that particular style of sardine tin has long since been superceded by the modern ring-pull, the underlying design problem remains unresolved. The ring-pull may make the task of opening the tin refreshingly easy but there is a terrible sting in the tail, for as the lid comes free of the container, it springs back, flicking tomato and olive oil onto the front of the cool shirt you've just changed into.

So the sardine tin remains a design problem whose solution momentarily eludes us. It's a case of a design scenario whose consequences - while irritating - are never sufficiently severe for anyone to be sufficiently 'arsed' to do anything about it.

Sardine tins - a retraction.

In response to my recent item on sardine tins a reader made the following observation:

> While I enjoyed your piece, I have to take exception to the description of the 4-6-0 Stanier as 'humble'. After all this was the class which included 'Sherwood Forester', 'Royal Scot' and 'Old Contemptibles'. The Walschaerts piston valves alone mark them out as superior machines.

It is gratifying to know that there are those amongst my readers who consider accuracy in these matters to be of vital importance. I stand corrected.

# Everyday design No. 2:
# Andrew's Salts

*To: GlaxoSmithKline*
*Consumer Healthcare*
*Re: Original Andrew's Salts*

Though I am only an occasional user of this product, I find it effective and always try to keep some to hand. All the same, the packaging of your product is without doubt one of the most extreme cases of bad design I have ever come across.

I refer to the plastic, oval bottle with the blue spoon attached to the lid.

I am taking the time to write about this because I am genuinely fascinated by the process that led to such a design being dreamed up, approved and put into production. It is not simply a matter of not being good, it is more a case of taking bad design to new heights. In short, the person who designed this packaging is clearly something of an evil genius.

Let's start at the top:

Firstly there's that spoon that you have to snap off to use. It is too short for a start. As soon as the level of the contents is down to around 80% they can no longer be reached by the spoon – which is probably a good thing, as it is stored in an exposed position on the top of the lid and liable to get dirty. What's more, the way the lid opens makes it almost inevitable that you will place the tip of your finger in the bowl of the spoon just prior to using it – not a good idea.

No, snap the spoon off and throw it away. It's worse than useless. To get at the contents you will need a very special kind of spoon. A teaspoon is too short. A desertspoon would be long enough but is too wide to use in the awkwardly shaped container. No – you will need to get yourself one of those long-handled, teaspoon-sized affairs used to eat Knickerbocker Glories in 1960s ice-cream parlours. You should keep one where you will be able to find it easily, in the middle of the night, when suffering from indigestion.

The lid is not easy to use either. On the face of it, it looks OK. There is a little depression in the end and a projecting tab for the thumb – but I always find myself trying a couple of other ways first. It is a problem that starts with that spoon. The lid moulding presents two or three distinct profiles that each looks like it might be the edge of the lid, together with intriguing tabs to try with your thumbnail.

It is difficult to believe that such a simple piece of packaging can be so rich in surprises. For example, I was astounded to read on the label on the back of the container:

*See inside label for how to open and dosage instructions.*

Am I to take this to mean that there is a second label, inside the container that gives you instructions on how to open it?

However, on the lower corner of the first label there is a triangular yellow tab bearing this amazing statement:

*Peel here but do not remove*

On carefully peeling back the corner of the label we find that there is a second, hidden label underneath, containing, amongst other things, advice on opening the container and correct use of the spoon. This must be the mysterious inside label referred to earlier.

All the same, as the advice is not to remove the outer label, I carefully lower it back in place.

In this age of technological marvels, of incomprehensible machines and processes, of expert design and professionalism, it is encouraging to come across something so bad as to be almost brilliant. It restores my faith in the imperfection of human nature.

Somewhere, in your organisation there is an exceptional individual, capable of the most bizarre and dysfunctional feats of design. If you are aware of any other examples of his (or her) work, I would be most interested to know of them.

Regards,

William Wormwood

... a week or two later I received a reply

Dear Mr Wormwood,

Thank you for your letter regarding your disappointment with the pack design of our Andrew's Salts. We are proud of our reputation for high quality and are sorry that we have not met your expectations on this occasion. As we are continually assessing our products with regard to packaging etc. we are grateful that you have gone to the trouble of letting us know your views.

Yours sincerely, [*illegible squiggle*]

Breaking news:

I note, on visiting my local pharmacy, that the Andrew's packaging remains essentially unchanged but that they have dispensed with the removable spoon. I like to think it was my allusions to the risk of bacterial contamination that prompted them to action.

All the same, I would have loved to discover more about that designer; I can't help fantasising that he or she was responsible the Dyson DC21:

# Everyday design No. 3: The Dyson DC21

When Dyson first launched its range of bagless vacuum cleaners I was given one in part payment for some design work and I loved it right from the start.

Well maybe 'love' is a bit too strong a word but it worked well enough and was almost a pleasure to use. It had one or two nice little qualities like an ability to perch halfway up the stairs and a tolerance for being dragged around by its hose at all sorts of angles. Otherwise it was charmingly devoid of complications.

Then, after some 12 years of hard, unsparing use, the motor - quite reasonably, in my opinion - decided to pack it in and I got it into my head to take it to the dump rather than to the local Vac Doctor, who I have since discovered could have had a replacement motor installed in no time.

But then secretly I had been eyeing up the later Dyson models and seduced by their distinctive looks, which reminded me of Giger's design for Alien, I went out and bought a brand new DC21.

The first thing that should be said about this machine is that it bites. I have been bitten on at least three occasions and always in sensitive parts of the body like between thumb and forefinger which suggests that the instruction manual should include a warning along the lines:

*On no account should this machine be used as a sex toy.*

All the same, in view of the risk of putting ideas into people's heads, a general caution relating to bite avoidance would probably be better.

The other peculiarity of the latest Dyson machines is that you can never be quite sure just what is attached to what and exactly how. Parts that look like they should be fixed on firmly give the impression that they are about to drop off while other components that you'd like to be able to get at easily, like the dust bucket, are fiendishly difficult to detach. You end up feeling that a diagram might be helpful, similar to the ones used to describe magic tricks with rope, and featuring hands, arrow symbols and dotted lines accompanied by words such as 'grasping the handle lightly with the second and third fingers of the right hand, press the button with the thumb while maintaining a steady pressure between the two components.'

You get the impression that the kids in the Dyson design department were given some expensive solid-modelling software and invited to *see what they could do with it*. And since they were probably fresh from modelling dragons or the like they proved they could do quite a lot.

The new Dyson doesn't perch on the stairs any more either. No doubt, after a number of accidents and accompanying claims for compensation in which the victim had been lulled into a false sense of security by the seemingly natural way in which the earlier version of the cleaner sat on the stairs, it was decided that the new model should be designed to encourage a healthy sense of insecurity.

Of course, what Dyson should do now is launch the DC24 'Alien' – which would be just like the other models but with a matt-black finish and special retracting mouthparts, for dealing with those extra tough cleaning challenges.

Now there's a machine you wouldn't want to mess around with.

# On suffering fools
# (gladly or otherwise)

After encountering it for what I swear must be the third or fourth time in as many days I am beginning to develop a deep aversion for the phrase

*'He was not one to suffer fools gladly.'*

along with its even more clichéd variant

*'... never one to suffer fools gladly.'*

It's that '*gladly*' that gets to me; I'd be quite content with a straightforward refusal to suffer fools full-stop; I'd find that perfectly reasonable - even though personally speaking I have nothing against them (fools that is).

But the '*gladly*' suggests that the person in question is quite prepared to suffer fools *through gritted teeth* or *with smouldering resentment* or suchlike - just not with anything approaching normal human decency.

The consequence is that, while I appreciate that the phrase is customarily trotted out to enhance a person's reputation, for me it has entirely the opposite effect - suggesting, instead, a somewhat mean-minded and ultimately insecure character.

No, when it comes to choosing which categories of people we might be unwilling to suffer - gladly or in any other way - I will opt for the self-satisfied, intolerant bigots every time.

Leave the fools alone - they're just fine.

# The Right to be wrong

*'Gonna make a mistake, gonna do it on purpose.'*
*Fiona Apple*

I have been thinking of that unmade bed that Tracy Emin exhibited at the Tate in 1999 and how it's often held up as the supreme example of subversive art.

Now the literal meaning of subvert is somewhere between undermine and overthrow and when it comes to overthrowing accepted artistic conventions or people's sense of decency I'd be the first to admit - you could do a lot worse than the Bed.

However, if it is the very fabric of society that you've set your sights on overthrowing, you're going to need something a little stronger, something like the Mischievous Calculator – an electronic calculator that makes mistakes.

Maybe it has happened already. Can you be really sure that the humble calculator that lies on your desk is entirely faithful in its operation? Our trust in such technologies is so complete that, even when faced with a clearly incorrect answer, we would almost certainly put it down to an error on our own part. We might repeat the calculation and this time, of course, it would be correct. It is the subtlety of the imperfection that is essential to the project.

To imbue a simple electronic calculator with an element of mischief is far from straightforward. A calculator that was merely defective would betray itself through degenerate behaviour. It might give an identical answer to every sum or refuse to display an answer at all. My mischievous calculator, on the other hand, will be entirely unpredictable in its failings. It might be a paragon of arithmetical perfection for years on end, before one day perversely declaring that 3x7=23. And when challenged to repeat its mistake, it will blithely revert to its former dependability.

The mischievous calculator will be significantly more complex than its well-behaved counterpart. To decide precisely how and in what circumstances the rules of arithmetic are to be perverted is a challenging design problem that will call for imagination and a high degree of inventiveness.

Once designed however, my calculator will be put on the market at a competitive price and, via a multitude of small, south-east Asian workshops, will find it's way to the four corners of the world, where it will do what is expected of it: in banks, bars, and brothels, faithfully executing mundane sums. Most of the time, at least.

Slowly however doubts will begin to take hold. Rumours will begin to circulate of a fundamental unreliability in arithmetic. Newspapers will report a spate of violent disputes over restaurant bills. Cases will be brought to court whose outcome will hinge on expert testimony to the effect that such things are impossible. The rumours will gradually subside - until the day, that is, when one of the rogue devices is identified and isolated, having been caught in the act, as it were. Analysed and dissected by experts, it is revealed to be perversely and deliberately flawed and, while dispelling the mystery, this revelation will simultaneously provoke a resurgence of mistrust.

Henceforth, every simple calculation will be open to

dispute. Old people who can recall how to do sums the old-fashioned way will be called as expert witnesses. Little children will be taught to chant their tables once again.

But this is just the start. Beyond the mischievous calculator other, more ambitious projects beckon: a temperamental mobile maybe - or a capricious computer. Both will entail technical challenges of an entirely new order of magnitude. Indeed, preliminary investigations indicate that nothing less than a form of artificial intelligence will be required – almost certainly of limited aptitude and with no more than simple cognitive powers, but nonetheless exhibiting an unmistakeable, if rudimentary, capacity for real naughtiness.

In his book, The Cyberiad, Stanislaw Lem tells the story of an inventor who constructs an intelligent machine which, when asked the ritual question: how much is two plus two, gives the defiant answer – seven. Repeated adjustments and tinkering with the mechanism does nothing to improve matters. Though the inventor is disappointed, his friend is not entirely unimpressed – declaring;

> '.... there is no question but that we have here a stupid machine, and not merely stupid in the usual, normal way, oh no! This is, as far as I can determine – and you know I am something of an expert – this is the stupidest thinking machine in the entire world, and that's nothing to sneeze at! To construct, deliberately, such a machine would be far from easy; in fact I would say that no one could manage it. For the thing is not only stupid, but stubborn as a mule.'

# Badgers

Having noted that badgers appear to be embarking on major subterranean engineering works in our garden, I decided to consult Google on what I might do to deter them. First thing that popped up was:

*'You should consider how fortunate you are to have these animals in your garden, despite any damage they may cause. There are a lot of people who would give anything to have their own garden badger sett.'*

All the same, the thought of a complex of dugouts, ditches and other military-style earthworks just a few yards from our back door is just the sort of thing that keeps me awake at night. Especially in view of the next piece of information I unearthed:

*'The Badger Protection Act 1992 forbids interference with badgers or their setts until a licence is granted by the government body, Natural England, with offenders risking a fine of up to £5,000 for each badger or sett affected.'*

But this is nothing, compared with the following seemingly innocuous advice:

*'... if badgers start to excavate a sett in your garden you should seek immediate help.'*

It is the ambiguity that is so alarming here. What sort of help are they talking about? Counselling, perhaps? Or is it something altogether darker that is being hinted at?

I find myself recalling a passage from Flann O'Brien's

The Plain People of Ireland. Rummaging through the bookcase, I find it:

*'... you'll find it's a badger you have in the house. Them lads would take the hand off you. Better go aisy now with them lads. Ate the face of you when you're asleep in the bed. Hump him out of the house before he has you destroyed man. Many's a good man had the neck off him by a badger. A good strong badger can break a man's arm with one blow of his hind leg, don't make any mistake about that. Show that badger the door.'*

But of course badgers are peaceful and shy creatures. What can I be thinking of? And we don't have them in the house (just yet). I should try keeping things in proportion.

All the same ....

# The Culture Secretary, Jeremy Hunt[1]

Listening to BBC presenters reporting on the culture secretary is a bit like watching show-jumping.

Sarah Montague, for instance, had a tricky round earlier this morning. Approaching the fence that has caused many a fine rider sleepless nights, she at first appeared supremely confident.

I have to confess my heart was in my mouth, as I sensed she was taking it too quickly.

Hooves drumming:

*the culture secretary Jeremy Hunt*
*the culture secretary Jeremy Hunt*
*the culture secretary Jeremy Hunt*

she approached the jump head on.

But then - just as I feared - she seemed to lose impulse at the critical moment and almost faltered.

As it turned out, her back hooves barely cleared the top rail.

Well done Sarah! Hurrah!

All the same - it was a heart-stopping moment.

---

[1] Written at the time of the famous Jeremy Hunt name curse that afflicted a number of BBC presenters including Jim Naughtie and Justin Webb.

# Chloe Smith MP

The sudden cancellation of the rise in fuel duty was defended on Channel 4 News and Newsnight by junior treasury minister Chloe Smith MP[1].

Personally, I don't think I have ever seen a better example of what might be termed the blocking interview technique, in which the aim is to stick resolutely to one's own ground and at all costs to avoid answering questions or confirming the interviewer's assertions, however innocent-seeming. And in this specialised skill I have to acknowledge Chloe Smith as something of an expert.

Anyway, it led me to speculate on behind the scenes conversations at the treasury:

It is Tuesday, 26th June and Chief Secretary to the Treasury, Danny Alexander summons rising star, Chloe Smith MP for a briefing:

**DA:** So Chloe, we have to put someone up against Paxman tonight. I'd do it myself but I have a parent's evening. It's a nuisance but I really can't get out of it. Anyway, I've been discussing it with George and we both think you're totally capable of handling this one.

**CS:** Oh thank you boss. If you think I can help then I'll give it all I've got.

**DA:** Brilliant! I felt sure we could rely on you. Now as you know, Paxman is a vicious bruiser. It's not going to be easy.

---

[1] 26 June, 2012

CS: Don't worry boss - I know what to do. I came top of my group in training and I'm ready to put it to work.

DA: Good girl. Show him what you're made of.

DA (Later on the phone to George Osborne): Well she's plucky - that's for sure. I just hope she's up to it.


At the Newsnight studios, later that evening - Chloe Smith MP is interviewed by the formidable Jeremy Paxman.

JP: So Mrs Smith, what time did you get up this morning?

CS: I slept very well thank you (as I always do) and found it very refreshing.

JP: I am sure we are all very pleased to hear that but that wasn't my question. My question was what time did you get out of bed this morning?

CS: My bed is very comfortable. It is a kingsize bed with a Hungarian goose down duvet.

JP: So it is clear that you did sleep last night and now here you are in the studio, so at some point in between you must have got up. Or is there some flaw in my reasoning?

CS: I am not here to comment on your reasoning; I am here to report on the fact that I had a deep and refreshing sleep.

JP: So if we can take it that you are no longer asleep right now then at some point since last night you must have woken up. When exactly was that Mrs Smith?

CS: What your viewers are more concerned with is the fact that, after a good night's sleep, I am here - awake, alert and working on their behalf.

JP: So you're not going to tell us what time you got up then?

CS: As I have said, I slept extremely well.

JP: Chloe Smith, thankyou.


DA (on the phone to George Osborne after the show): Wasn't she great? Wow! Told you George. What a performance! Might be an idea for you to give her a call and thank her personally George. You know - she's hungry and ambitious and up for anything I reckon.

GO: You're right Danny. We're going to need her again.

# A souvenir of Venice

Whenever I go away for more than a day or two I like to seek out a special object, delicacy or suchlike to bring back home with me. If I go up to Lancashire, for example, there's a very good chance I'll come back with a black pudding. On one occasion, having been seduced by the intoxicating delights of Stockport covered market, I brought some tripe back, in the belief that some deep Lancashire part of me would instinctively know how to go about eating it. It didn't.

Thinking further afield – each destination offers its own unique and fascinating souvenirs.

In Hong Kong you can buy a bottle of wine with a dead snake coiled up inside it. At first it might seem an ideal souvenir -- at least until you have the presence of mind to realise that, in some desperate or tormented state, you might be driven to drink it.

Venice presents its own peculiar difficulties in the souvenir department. To kick-off, there are the carnival masks: a variety of pale courtesans and that other one with a long, drooping proboscis – or is it a beak? But then what would you honestly want to do with a carnival mask?

'I could wear it at parties' you find yourself thinking. But then you know for sure that, when it comes to it, it will never be exactly right. And what else is there to do with a pair of carnival masks other than to mount them at a jaunty tilt on either side of the chimney breast?

No - the carnival masks won't do.

Glass? Since the thirteenth century Venice has produced a steady stream of exquisite glassware - most of which has since been accidentally broken. Today the descendants of those early glassmakers churn out a dazzling variety of objects, mainly ghastly, except for the chandeliers which -- you may confidently have it from me -- are gorgeous.

I briefly toyed with the idea of buying one of those chandeliers, despite the fact that they can cost as much as a decent secondhand car. This is in Venice, of course. I have since seen the self-same items online for a fraction of the Venice price. But hey, hang on: this is beginning to sound like one of those nightmare conversations you hear about prices whilst queuing up to be let back into your country. I am *meant* to be thinking about souvenirs and whether glass might do ... and no, it won't.

There are nice paper-style goods in Venice. There's lovely wrapping paper printed with Rococo designs and if I were to buy some, I would take it home and I would squirrel it away carefully; and later, after my death, my children would discover it and, later, recount to others: 'There were drawers and drawers full of exquisite Venetian wrapping paper. I don't know whether he planned to do anything with it or whether he just enjoyed it for its beauty. It broke our hearts to take it to the recycling.'

So that's the paper out as well.

In the end it was a hat.

Right from the start of our holiday, on the waterbus that carries you across the lagoon from the airport, I had noted that our driver was wearing an interesting woolly hat that would have been a perfect fit had his head been the shape of a rugby ball. As it was a normal head, the empty, surplus bit of hat was left to droop backwards in a manner that invoked images of generations of lagoon-dwellers, netting wildfowl on damp, misty mornings.

So the hat it had to be.

Finding it proved to be harder than I first imagined - the problem being, it wasn't a tourist item. But then, having to track it down, scouring the outdoor markets and department stores that somehow manage to cling on to the less fashionable fringes of the city, lent the whole quest an extra level of romance. I found one at last, hanging outside a hardware store and costing about 5 euros and for the rest of our holiday enjoyed swaggering around the decks of waterbuses in the hope of being mistaken for a deckhand who had just finished his shift and was on his way home.

I still have it. It's a nice hat.

# The English language

As everyone knows, William Shakespeare was a one for the words. In fact he is considered something of a specialist in that particular department -- having a vocabulary of some 17,677 separate words at his disposal.

Now the Oxford English Dictionary (20 volumes, £750, Oxford University Press) contains 218,632 different words and this has got me thinking: imagine getting 12 Elizabethan playwrights together in a room. You could share out all the words in the dictionary between them and they'd each end up with more than enough to produce a decent lifetime's work. And here's the best bit: not one of them would be able to understand a single word written by any of the others.

All of which gives me an idea: namely to frame this otherwhile evagation with such fienden cautel, meandriform tortuosity and wanhopely intertanglements that even keenly philologues won't have the faintest clue as to what I'm on about.

And while the most pertinatious might be forgiven for renouncing exigent or otherwise usitative obligements only to prove susceptive to pococurantish musardry -- especially late at night, after a glass of wine or two -- the rorty ribaldise that later survenes when, having thumbled the hirpled visure of semblesse, they eagerly forsake the embrace of Morpheous for the sweeter allures of Venus -- well it doesn't bear thinking about.

# The Deference Engine

As every fool knows, if you want to write a letter to the Queen, you start it with

*May it please Your Majesty*

And on the envelope, the first line of the address should read

*Her Majesty The Queen*

If, on the other hand, it is the Prince of Wales who is to be the beneficiary of your insight and advice, you should open the letter with a straightforward Your Royal Highness, while addressing the envelope

*HRH The Prince of Wales.*

So far, so good. The complications come when wishing to petition some of the more exotic species to be found amongst the English aristocracy. For example, let us imagine for a moment that you are the tenant of a marquess and that you wish to write him a letter begging to be relieved of some feudal obligation.

You might start the letter with *My Lord Marquess* and address the envelope:

*The Most Hon The Marquess of Whatever*

OR, alternatively

*The Most Hon The Marquess Whatever*

But only one of these is right and it depends on some obscure rules. While attempting to clarify the matter you might unearth the following guidance:

*It (the 'of', that is) may be omitted in the form of Marquessates and Earldoms and included in the form of Scottish Viscountcies. It is never present in peerage Baronies and Lordships of Parliament and always present in Dukedoms and Scottish feudal Baronies.*

All of which -- let us admit it -- is as clear as mud. Get it wrong however and your carefully crafted letter is likely to find itself cast, unopened, onto the fire.

In the case of the marquesses it seems there is little alternative other than to work your way, one by one, through the entire list in order to discover whether, in your particular case, the 'of' should be included or not.

Which is precisely what I was assigned to do during one of the more unusual jobs I did 'back in the day'. Having been taken on by a small, one-man company contracted to construct the mailing lists for DeBretts Peerage and Baronetage (available from all good booksellers -- £100), my job was to work through all the names and addresses in order to ensure that, in the automatically generated mailshots, begging letters and so on, the recipients would find themselves addressed as befitted their station.

However, as is well known, computer programmers are reputed for their laziness. Rather than spend half a lifetime verifying the correct form of address for the entire aristocracy, not to mention the upper ranks of the armed forces, members of the judiciary and senior clerics, it struck me that the entire process could be better done by an algorithm. After all there are rules and a set of rules is all that is needed in these cases.

Nevertheless, some of the rules are fairly complex.

Take this, for example:

> *If the definite article is not used before courtesy peerages and The Hon Elizabeth Smith marries Sir William Brown, she becomes The Hon Lady Brown, but if she marries the higher-ranked Lord Brown, a courtesy Baron, she becomes only Lady Brown. If this Sir William Brown's father is created Earl of London and Baron Brown, as a result of this enoblement, his wife's style will actually change, from 'The Hon Lady Brown' to 'Lady Brown'. It is important to note that while the style may appear diminished, the precedence taken increases from that of the wife of a knight to that of the wife of an earl's eldest son.*

And quite right too, I say.

However, when the time came to embark on implementing my project, it was sadly one of those cases where the anticipated volume of sales (paltry) was unlikely to justify the projected development effort (significant) and I had no alternative but to set it aside.

All the same, it was worth it just for the name:

The Deference Engine

# Dreaming of the seaside

July 2020

It might have been the sound of wind in the treetops that recently evoked this vivid recollection of the seaside.

Every time I lie, face-down on a sandy beach I return to the same place -- a tiny place bounded by my own face and folded arms; a cool, sheltered and shady den from where, behind half-closed eyes, I watch the breeze stirring tiny flurries of sand in the light filtering in from the sunny beach.

The tiny hairs on my forearms bristle with quiet energy; I smell salt on my skin.

As if from deep within a seashell, I hear the rhythmic breathing of the sea as it touches the shore. The shouts of excited children are all mingled with the waves. From further along, by the water's edge, a dog barks.

# ABOUT THE AUTHOR

David Wilson has lived in the village of Horsley, Gloucestershire for the past 34 years. He has a wide-ranging set of interests.

In 2012 he walked from Lands End to Cape Wrath in NW Scotland.

Printed in Great Britain
by Amazon